RAY ILLINGWORTH

RAY
ILLINGWORTH

The Tempestuous Years
1979–83

RAY ILLINGWORTH
with
Steve Whiting

SIDGWICK & JACKSON
LONDON

First published in Great Britain in 1987
by Sidgwick & Jackson Limited

Copyright © 1987 Ray Illingworth

ISBN 0-283-99386-3

Photoset by Rowland Phototypesetting Ltd,
Bury St Edmunds, Suffolk
Printed in Great Britain by Butler & Tanner Limited,
Frome, Somerset
for Sidgwick & Jackson Limited
1 Tavistock Chambers, Bloomsbury Way
London WC1A 2SG

CONTENTS

LIST OF PLATES

Ray Illingworth

Ian Botham and Co. (*Action-Plus*)
Ian Botham (*Associated Sports Photography*)
Me (*Patrick Eagar*)
Brian Johnston (*Patrick Eagar*)
Radio team (*Patrick Eagar*)
Me 'before' (*Patrick Eagar*)
Me 'after' (*Associated Sports Photography*)

FINDING MY VOICE

It's taken me three years to come round to writing this book. Three years to bring myself to say one thing I know must be said, yet at the same time breaks my heart even to think about. And that's this: 'I'm damned glad I no longer have anything at all to do with Yorkshire County Cricket Club.'

Bear with me and you will learn, probably for the first time, exactly what went on at Yorkshire during those five fiery years between 1979 and 1983 when I was their manager. And don't think I'll be coming in off my short run – I believe in telling the truth, even if it hurts. Things might have turned out so differently for Yorkshire if there had been more men around with the same attitude during those troubled years. There have been enough lies told already. I'm not about to add to them.

Looking back, I reckon it was the skulduggery, the scheming and the downright dishonesty that sickened me most. We Yorkies have always been proud of our honesty and integrity – qualities that were drummed into me so hard they became almost second nature from the very first day I ever played for Yorkshire – in a Championship game (what else was there in those days?) against Hampshire at Headingley in 1951 when I was a skinny, nervous lad of nineteen. Norman Yardley was captain then. He was chairman of the England selectors as well – a firm man, but a warm one. Perhaps it was no coincidence that in those days Yorkshire was the best team in the land. And even if they did bicker among themselves and make life hell for anyone who was not pulling his weight, they soon closed ranks if anyone from outside tried to knock them. That was what impressed me about the 1950 Tykes – their loyalty – and there was precious little of that left when I went back in 1979.

Of course, I knew nothing of that in the summer of 1977 when Michael Crawford, at that time the club's treasurer, rang to ask if I was interested in leaving Leicestershire, where I had spent ten very happy years, to go back to Yorkshire as manager for the following season. I liked Leicester, so did my wife Shirley and daughters Vicky and Diane. Yet the call from Mr Crawford really came as no surprise as there had been quite a deal of press speculation on the subject and, after all, the green, green Dales of Yorkshire were still home. So before I knew it I was in the Metropole Hotel in the middle of Leeds, sipping a beer with Mr Crawford and hoping nobody would see us.

Back in Leicester Shirley and I made quite a contribution to the profits of Brooke Bond as we drank cup after cup of tea before coming to our decision. We had many friends in Leicester, and I had seen the county grow from a team where visiting players always took their golf clubs in the hope of a few hours off on the third day into a side with the likes of young David Gower to make the games both exciting and entertaining. I also had the promise from secretary Mike Turner that when my playing days were over there would always be a job for me at Grace Road. But once a Yorkie, always a Yorkie – how I wish I had known then what I know now. But I didn't – so I rang Michael Crawford and told him, 'OK, I'm coming back' – after I had honoured my contract with Leicester which had one more year to run.

So, in 1979 began five years that were, at their best, interesting, and at their worst, especially for my wife and daughters, downright frightening. But that's history now – as much part of the past as the Wars of the Roses. And when I look around at the peace and the pleasure I enjoy now it's hard to believe they ever really happened. For the bad times are slowly fading, but nothing will ever erase completely the memories of what went on at Yorkshire between 1979 and 1983. I just hope that by telling it now I may be able to prevent anything like it ever tearing that great county apart in that way ever again.

1
RETURN TO YORKSHIRE

Geoffrey Boycott (Boycs) was involved in my spell – or should I say sentence? – as manager of Yorkshire right from the very start. No, that's not strictly true; he was involved, or tried to be, before I had even as much as a notion that the job might one day be offered to me.

Nobody had spoken to me about the Yorkshire managership and all I knew was what anyone else who read the Yorkshire papers knew – that the county might, and only might, appoint a manager, and that I was one of the men they were interested in. So you can imagine my surprise when, one summer afternoon in 1977, our front-door bell rang and there was Geoffrey Boycott with Ann Wyatt, his faithful, long-time lady friend.

'We were on our way to Harrogate, so we thought we'd drop in,' said Geoffrey. So why should I be surprised? We had, after all, known each other a long time and we did share one great common interest in cricket. And Pudsey was on the way from Leeds to Harrogate and I'm sure Geoffrey was aware that I did go back there sometimes when I had a couple of days off from cricket in Leicester. Only Geoffrey had never been to my home before that moment and I can promise you he has never been there since. So why now? Naturally there would be plenty for two cricketers to chew the fat over but Boycott never drops in just for a chat.

This was the year Geoffrey had chosen to return to the Test arena after being absent since the 1974–5 tour of Australia.

Many people think he gave that tour a miss because Mike Denness had been made captain with John Edrich as his number two, and I think there is a lot in what they say. But on the day he came to my house I don't think he had yet made his memorable comeback against the Aussies at Trent Bridge which was towards the end of July. By the same token he had yet to make his one hundredth century against them – that came a fortnight later in the Test at Headingley. I feel that if he had already done those things, the talk may never have got round to the Yorkshire managership. But gradually the subject just seemed to crop up as we discussed what had been in the papers and what people had been saying – you know, general chit-chat.

Then a strange thing happened which, though it was all of ten years ago, is etched on my memory as clearly as if it was only yesterday. As the pair of them were about to leave Ann stood up and said these exact words: 'Geoffrey with a manager. Over my dead body!'

At the time I didn't think too much about it. After all, that phone call from Michael Crawford inviting me to Leeds for a chat hadn't even arrived at this stage and I had no idea I was really in line for the job. Looking back now I can see that Ann had summed up the situation in a nutshell. I did become Geoffrey's manager. And there were quite a few dead bodies to be stepped over – not only Ann's!

I'm sure Geoffrey and Ann had talked over all the speculation that had been going on and had agreed that a job as manager of Yorkshire would be right up his street – almost made for him, you might say. One thing did become clear in the next few years – Boycott sure as hell didn't want anyone else to succeed in the job.

Yet it was all so silly . . . such a tragedy. At the time I had nothing personal against Boycott whatsoever, and even during the next few years, when the in-fighting was at its fiercest, I felt he must have been ashamed of some of the deeds that were being perpetrated in his name. After all, I'd been at Leicester since 1969 and the most I'd seen of him had been on the one England tour we had shared – that great

Ashes-winning series in Australia in 1970–1. Colin Cowdrey was my vice captain on that tour, an appointment I was not entirely happy with. It had been thrust on me while I was still getting my breath back at the end of an innings against the Rest of the World at Edgbaston. Chief selector Alec Bedser hit me with the decision in the dressing room almost before I had time to sit down – not the ideal moment to take up 'Big Al' on his demand to know if I was happy with their choice. All I could do was mutter 'Yes, I suppose so,' and before I could give it any serious thought, Cowdrey's appointment had been announced to the press and that was that.

Really, I don't think the selectors had used a lot of the old grey matter when they chose Colin as my vice captain. They must have known that he and I had not exactly been bosom buddies on Ted Dexter's tour to Australia in 1962–3 when Colin was also vice captain.

Cowdrey fell into the habit on that tour of turning up to the nets whenever the fancy took him and seemed to expect the bowlers, who may have been toiling away in the heat for an hour already, to feel delighted at the prospect of bowling to him for another half an hour. I told him that in Yorkshire when we say nets at 10 o'clock, that means 10 o'clock, not anything up to an hour later. I was fined £50 off my tour bonus, along with Barry Knight and Fred Trueman. To this day I don't know why I had my money stopped – but I suspect it may have had something to do with speaking my mind to our unpunctual vice captain.

Anyway, that was the way I felt about Cowdrey – and I did have another man in mind . . . Geoffrey Boycott. I was well aware of his faults. But I was also well aware of his strong points, and I truly feel that if Boycott could have served under me as vice captain on that tour, and perhaps for another two or three seasons afterwards, England would have found themselves a ready-made captain for almost as long as they needed him.

The mind simply boggles when you think of the difference that might have made to the course of English cricket. Boycott already possessed a deep knowledge of the game,

7

picked up largely because he always had to work at it. He never had the natural talent of a Gower or a Botham, but lessons learned the hard way are the ones that are more likely to stick.

I am certain Geoffrey would never have ruled himself out of Test cricket the way he did for three years if he had been captain – and what a difference that would have made to so many careers. He made himself unavailable from 1974 and did not say he was ready to play again until 1977. The selectors then made him wait until the third Test against Australia, at Nottingham, in July, when he made a century. He has never really said why he went into exile. Several explanations have been put forward – the favourite being that Mike Denness was made England captain in the West Indies in early 1974, and in Australia in 1974–5.

Knowing Geoffrey's fanaticism for personal fitness, something which I totally admire and applaud in Boycott, he might still have been leading England and piling up the records along the way. It's reasonable to assume that Mike Denness, Tony Greig, Mike Brearley, Ian Botham, Keith Fletcher and Bob Willis would have led them on no more than the odd occasion when Geoffrey was hurt or ill and perhaps only recently would David Gower and Mike Gatting have started to think: 'The old devil must pack it in soon . . . then perhaps I'll be given a go.'

It could have been a period of true stability for England – something akin to the continuity Clive Lloyd brought to the West Indies for so long. We would have missed the subtleties of Brearley, who might never even have played for England, as well as the riproaring 'Up Guards and at 'em' approach of Greig. But if I have one overwhelming reason to be glad that Boycott failed to make the job his own, it is that his absence gave Keith Fletcher (Fletch) that chance of glory, albeit brief and cruelly cut off, when he led England on their tour of India in 1981–2. I felt sorry the selectors were in such a hurry to get rid of Fletch once that tour was over – even though he had shown his loyalty by refusing to have anything to do with the rebel trip to South

Africa which was brewing while the tour was in progress.

If I have a soft spot for little Fletch, it may be because there is a constant reminder of him on the shelf at my home in Pudsey – one of the mementoes left there after a series of raids by local burglars, obviously Yorkies, with insatiable appetites for cricket memorabilia. It is a cricket ball, mounted on the top of three little stumps – and thereby hangs a tale.

I'm told it was 12.36 p.m. on the fifth day of the seventh Test at the Sydney Cricket Ground in February 1971 that Fletch brought to an end the longest series of all time when he picked up Terry Jenner off the bowling of Derek Underwood to give us victory by 62 runs and with it those Ashes. As people grabbed stumps, bails and anything else they could lay their hands on, Fletch quietly slipped the ball into my hand and said, 'You have this, Skip. I reckon you deserve it.'

That was the match I took my team off the field after the crowd had attacked John Snow, that was the series when, in seven Tests, we didn't get one single lbw decision. It was the end of a five-month slog which was made even longer when it was decided to play another Test at Melbourne after the first had been washed out without a single ball bowled. It goes without saying that that dusty old Kookaburra ball is my most treasured keepsake – thanks to one Keith Fletcher.

So here we were in the middle of the 1977 season, and neither I nor Geoffrey Boycott knew for sure what the future held. In any case, I still had another year of my contract with Leicestershire to run, so my subsequent talks with Michael Crawford, my discussions with Shirley, and eventually my acceptance of Yorkshire's offer, all seemed geared to something rather distant and remote. My prime concern was with Leicestershire where I can honestly say, now I look back, I spent the happiest ten years of my cricket life. If there was any disappointment at the end of the 1977 season, it was that David Gower was overlooked for the winter tour to Pakistan and New Zealand. I've heard it said that Mike Brearley felt David was too young and raw at the time, but I wish he had spoken to me about him first, because I felt that, even then, at the age of only twenty, he was easily good enough.

Be that as it may, the upshot was that whatever was going on at Yorkshire during 1977 it had absolutely nothing to do with me. Naturally theirs was the first result I looked for in the paper – especially after I knew I was likely to be going back there some time as their manager. So it was only as an outsider that I read of the efforts being made by Don Brennan, the former Yorkshire and England wicket-keeper, to have Boycott removed from the captaincy and replaced by Geoff Cope, the England off-spinner, whose suspect action caused him to miss the next season and a year later to be thrown out of cricket altogether.

My involvement did not become public knowledge until 9 November 1977 when a committee meeting at Headingley announced that I was to be manager of Yorkshire from April 1979, when my contract with Leicestershire expired, and that Boycott was to remain captain for 1978. That was no concern of mine . . . in 1978 I would still be with Leicestershire. I was sorry, though, to hear that Brennan, an honest and decent worker for Yorkshire, had resigned from the committee after the decision to keep Boycott. The astute observer could have been in no doubt – the storm clouds were already gathering.

I believe a few people on the committee were a little disgruntled about the way my appointment had been made without consulting them. Fair enough. But that's the way it had to be and if there was any secrecy involved, then I am prepared to shoulder some of the blame. I felt it was the right approach . . . I hate watching football clubs conduct their business through the newspapers, and that wasn't Yorkshire's way.

I did the bulk of my negotiating on the telephone with Michael Crawford and then I met him, chairman Arthur Connell and Norman Shuttleworth to iron out the details. To have let it go any further at that time would have meant involving thirty or forty people and that, as I have since found to my cost and embarrassment, is as good as telling the whole of Yorkshire – if not the whole of England.

2

THE BIRTH OF
THE REFORM GROUP

By the winter of 1977–8 there was only one cloud on Geoffrey Boycott's horizon . . . me! Otherwise he must have been in his element. That summer had seen his re-emergence as a major Test player and he had the Yorkshire public solidly behind him after choosing Leeds to make his one hundredth first-class century. By the time of the news of his reappointment as captain – and anything less would have caused a riot at the time – he was packing his bags for the England tour of Pakistan and New Zealand, a tour that culminated in his one and only spell as England captain. But already I was worried; how much had Boycs learned about team spirit and self-sacrifice during the time I'd been away? And my mind kept gong back to one incident during that summer of 1977 – the moment he ran out local hero Derek Randall (Arkle) in the first innings of that third Test at Nottingham when he made his now legendary comeback.

Geoffrey gave it all the drama he could muster as little Arkle made his way back to the pavilion – bat thrown on the ground in anguish, head buried in his hands in despair. But I've looked at the video of that moment many times to make sure I wasn't imagining anything – and I wasn't. There it is every time; Geoffrey gives a quick glance to make sure the throw has gone to Randall's end, he makes double sure of his own safety with a quick grounding of the bat, and then come the histrionics. No, Geoffrey hadn't changed.

There's little doubt, either, that as he set off for Pakistan,

11

Geoffrey would have been aware of the birth of the Reform Group, brought into being largely by the anti-Boycott campaign led by Don Brennan. If they had known Boycott was going to come out on top in that little squabble and keep the captaincy for the following season, the Reform Group might never have come into being – and what a lot of problems Yorkshire would have been spared. As it was, they jumped the gun by one month.

In October 1977 Peter Briggs, one of the group's leading stirrers, called John Featherstone, a local government officer in Leeds, who was a nice-enough fellow I knew quite well. At that time I had never heard of Briggs, or Sid Fielden, or any of the other Reformers. Within a year I was beginning to wish I never had. Briggs, who was a Yorkshire member even though he worked as an accountant in Manchester, got really stirred up when he heard Brennan say on Radio Leeds: 'Geoff Boycott is a great player, but to my way of thinking he is not a leader. A captain should, in my opinion, be able to sacrifice himself, his own game, for the benefit of his side.'

In time to come I was to agree with Brennan. It was a shrewd and simple summary of Geoffrey's problems as a captain. But Brennan's remarks infuriated Boycott's fans and, as I have said, he had plenty of those by the end of the summer of 1977. Briggs and Featherstone called a meeting at the George Hotel in Huddersfield, a proper hotbed of revolution since, according to my BBC colleague Don Mosey, that is where the breakaway Rugby League was formed in 1895. Featherstone became secretary of the Reform Group and was active in some of their early campaigning. I'm simply happy to say that John was sensible and decent enough to quit the Group when he eventually saw the direction they were taking.

It wasn't long before the letters' columns of the Yorkshire papers, no doubt stirred up by Brennan's remarks, were overflowing with the opinions of the Reformers, even though many of them were disguised as coming from ordinary folk. This was the start of a letter-writing campaign that exploded like a bomb when the action really hotted up at the end of 1978 when Geoffrey did finally have the captaincy taken away – bringing to an end the ceaseless battles between him and the committee. But it was the events of 1978 which led up to that day that created the crux of the conflict between me and the Reformers. And I am now happy to have the chance to put them into their true and proper perspective.

I was still captain of Leicestershire in 1978 and that was where my professional loyalties lay, even though I knew by then that the following season would see me heading back to Headingley. I had a sneaking suspicion that the Yorkshire committee, though they had backed down in the face of opposition from the new Reformers, were still looking for the chance to rid themselves of Boycott as captain.

The Reform Group had presented the committee with a petition, signed by 828 members, declaring that there would be trouble if Boycott was fired. Even chairman Arthur Connell had described Brennan's campaign as 'deplorable' – but I now see that as a weak-kneed effort to keep the peace rather than face the truth, something that I was to see more and more of as the battle wore on. So it was no more than natural that I was starting to develop a nagging feeling that the committee were bringing me in so that I could, amongst other things, do what they did not have the guts to do – that is to fire their bullets at Boycott for them when they found they did not have the gumption to do it for themselves.

Yorkshire had won only 6 out of 21 Championship matches in 1977, and finished twelfth in the table (though Boycott was away for three Tests), so I was eagerly looking forward to Leicester's match against them at Grace Road in early June. Perhaps it was providence that brought Yorkshire down to Leicester minus Geoffrey, who had injured a thumb playing in a Prudential one-day international against Pakistan at Old Trafford. So Yorkshire were skippered by Jack Hampshire (Hamps) – and what a cracking game of cricket we had. They won by 4 wickets with 8 balls to spare after I had set them 271 to win in 57 overs. And they went for them from the word 'go' with Richard Lumb and Bill Athey setting them on their way with a brilliant opening stand of 189.

I now understand that some of the Yorkshire players, particularly the younger ones who didn't know me all that well, asked Boycott and Hampshire to get together with me and sort out a few matters for the following season. As it worked out, of course, Boycs wasn't there, so Hamps, who is an old pal of mine and still stays with me in Spain whenever he gets the chance, had dinner with me – just the two of us.

In the course of our chat I mentioned that Boycott had told me he didn't completely trust Hamps. Now Jack is the kind of guy who finds it almost impossible to see malice in anyone and, though this was far from being my intention, I think this was the beginning of the breakdown in relations between them.

At least that dinner gave me the chance to spell out to one senior Yorkshire player, and through him to all the others, what my methods would be when I became their manager. In November 1977, a couple of days after my appointment, I told the *Yorkshire Post*: 'I will be in charge and I will have the final say on all cricket matters, including team selection.' I think this rankled with Boycott because in some ways our views differed – particularly as to the bowling make-up of a team. Geoffrey usually favoured seam bowlers in one-day cricket whereas I, naturally, had more faith in the spinners than he did.

This made Geoffrey a little anxious, so we arranged a meeting at Headingley with about four or five other people – I can remember Norman Yardley, Michael Crawford and John Temple being amongst them. It worried Geoffrey when they confirmed that I was in sole charge of picking the team. I told him I realized I was keener on spinners than he was for the limited-over stuff, but I thought that if we talked it over we could work it out without any real problems. I told him that if I wanted to be awkward I could pick twelve players and make sure two of them were spinners so he would have to play one of them whether he liked it or not. But I added that we had both played cricket for a long time and I didn't see that as the way either of us would want to sort things out and we should discuss anything that arose in the light of our understanding of the game.

Geoffrey had to agree with that since the terms of my appointment had already been clearly stated. But it certainly didn't make him any happier with the state of affairs as he saw them. Obviously, what with me playing for Leicestershire and Geoffrey with either England or Yorkshire, we did not see a lot of each other in 1978. So there was little chance of much friction, even if one of us had wanted any – which I certainly know I didn't, and I don't think Geoffrey did either at that stage. But friction was always there – even if at times it merely bubbled away beneath the surface.

Though I wasn't there to see it at first hand, I am in no doubt that Jack Hampshire was still seething at being told that Boycott did not trust him when, exactly a month later, he staged his now famous 'go-slow' at Northampton when he and Colin Johnson put on only 11 runs in the final 10 overs of their first innings and so missed the fourth batting point. It took the next seven years for the truth to come out about the meetings that followed – whether Hampshire was reprimanded, whether he was warned, or whatever. Of two things I am certain: once again the Yorkshire committee made a complete fist of their handling of the affair and Hampshire's action had been his own way of telling the world that if Boycott thought he had a God-given right to bat at whatever speed he chose, then so did he.

It didn't look too good. But the way I saw things that summer of 1978, though I can already hear hollow, disbelieving laughter from some of the Reformers, was that I had been appointed cricketing manager of a county club that already had Geoffrey Boycott as their captain. There was nothing I could or should do to try and change that. My job was to assess the situation and only then would I be able to suggest changes. Unfortunately, or perhaps fortunately, events like the matches at Leicester and then Northampton began to establish a pattern well before I arrived and to daub the writing on the wall in ever larger letters.

The first hint of the problems to come had already arisen with Geoffrey and Ann's visit to my house, and then the need to spell out to him that I was going to be the boss and that I, not him, would be picking the teams – the 1st XI, 2nd XI and the Under-25s as well.

Then came another clue as to what life with Geoffrey was going to be like. He resented my appointment over him – fair enough, but there was no doubt about the way he felt. And it came out some time in 1978 when he asked me point-blank: 'How would you have liked it if Leicestershire had appointed a manager over you?' I said that if I had gone eight years as captain, as he had done, and not won anything, I would have accepted a manager with grace. I had been at Leicester for only three years when we won something, plus the fact that when I took over there I had told them I wanted a reasonably free hand, always accepting that if things didn't go well and they felt I wasn't the right man for the job, I would see out my contract and play to the best of my ability under any man they cared to put in charge and give him absolutely loyal service.

But at Leicester, of course, we did win things and I think winning became a habit, whereas at Yorkshire losing was rapidly becoming the norm. Success and failure are both habits and we got into the winning frame of mind at Leicester when we took the Benson & Hedges Cup in 1972, my third year with the club, after going ninety-three years without a touch. After that, until I left at the end of 1978, Leicestershire won the Benson & Hedges Cup again and reached the final once more, won the John Player League twice and, above all, took their first County Championship pennant in 1975.

3

DRAWING UP THE BATTLE LINES

If Boycott's challenge had been a hint, the next thing to take place was most definitely a bash straight between the eyes and something had to be done about it before I took over at Yorkshire the following season. A lot of misunderstanding has arisen about the players' poll and the letter I wrote to Yorkshire chairman, Arthur Connell, when I got wind of it. At last I have the chance to put the record straight.

Even though I was still in my last season at Leicester and a good few miles down the M1, I would have needed to be a polar bear living on an ice floe not to have known that Boycott's captaincy was causing a fair amount of unrest at Yorkshire, particularly amongst the players. I knew it was a problem that would have to be sorted out one day – one way or another. But what I then heard on the cricket grapevine told me that things had gone as far as could be tolerated. What I heard was that off-spinner Geoff Cope – a nice, decent, family lad who wanted little more than to be able to enjoy his cricket in a congenial atmosphere – had conducted a round robin amongst the Yorkshire players to ask whether they wanted Geoffrey as captain. It has been suggested in some places – and by now you may well be able to guess where – that in some way I instigated this poll.

Well, that is totally untrue. I didn't even hear of it until it had already taken place. But when I did, I had to ring Cope and ask him if it was true. He said it was and that, what's more, according to his poll, 95 per cent of the capped players

17

did not want Geoffrey as skipper! Once I found that out I was in a funny position because I still feel, and I'm not certain if I'm right or wrong, that if 95 per cent of the players don't want you as captain there is no way you are going to be successful. I don't think I, personally, would want to do the captain's job if 95 per cent of the lads didn't want me. I'd say, 'OK, I'll play on, and whoever you want as captain can do it.' They've got to want you as captain or it can't work. It's impossible.

I didn't want this sort of thing still simmering when I started back at Yorkshire. So I wrote a letter to the chairman saying, 'Look, I think this matter should be straightened out before I come back. I don't want aggravation like this on my hands the moment I get back, so please sort it out.'

By all accounts the Reform Group held this against me because they felt this swayed the committee when it met in September to discuss the question of the captaincy for the following season – my first as manager. At the end of that meeting secretary Joe Lister was called upon to read out another momentous statement in the name of Yorkshire CCC. It said:

> *The Yorkshire County Cricket Club, after long and careful consideration, have decided that the interests of the club would best be served by offering the captaincy to J. H. Hampshire. The committee very much hope that Geoff Boycott will continue to extend his valuable services as a player and have offered him a two-year contract to continue as such. They are grateful to him for what he has done for the club over many years and as captain over the last eight years.*

The Reform Group went mad. And they were even madder when my letter was read out at a special meeting which they forced at the Royal Hall, Harrogate, in December, in an effort to make the committee reinstate Boycott as captain. They were convinced my letter had influenced the committee in September and later at the Harrogate meeting when members backed the committee by 4,422 votes to 3,067, thanks largely to 3,952 proxy votes. The majority in favour of sacking Boycott and bringing in Jack Hampshire was even wider – 4,826 against 2,602. But the Reformers were wrong. All I had asked the committee to do was to sort out the matter one way or the other before I went back. How they did it was up to them. I knew I would have enough on my hands when I took up my duties and I did not want to have this problem hanging over me, especially as I knew the committee could and should grasp the nettle and settle it.

But the Reform Group were well and truly on my back – and I hadn't even started! They felt that without my letter they would have carried the day at Harrogate, but they were wrong. After ten years away I was being treated to a very short, sharp reminder of how high feelings can run in Yorkshire. As Bill Shankly once said of his love of football: 'It's not a matter of life and death. It's much more important than that.' The Tyke feels the same about his cricket.

I have to admit this was a bad time for Boycott. And I felt sorry for him. But I will not stand for some of the innuendoes he and certain of his friends indulged in at that time. On 4 September, the England party to tour Australia was named, with Bob Willis, and not Boycott, vice captain under Mike Brearley. And on 25 September his dear old mum, Mrs Jayne Boycott, who had brought Geoffrey up ever since his dad died when he was a lad, passed away after a long illness.

Geoffrey, like most cricketers at the end of a long season, was away on holiday at the time. He was called home and arrived at the little house he and his mother shared in Fitzwilliam to find a letter from the county asking him to attend a selection committee meeting on 22 September. That had clearly long passed, but as soon as the letter was sent, the county, realizing Geoffrey was away, sent another one changing the date to 28 September. By that time, of course, all selection matters concerned me as well, since I was due to take over the following April, and I was being kept in touch with what was going on. So I know that 28 September was no good to Geoffrey either since that was the day he actually arrived home. The date was pushed back by one more day – to the 29th. It is now that the facts start to become a little clouded and some of the Reformers began to show, as far as I could see, that there were not many tricks that they would not stoop to.

The Yorkshire committee came in for a lot of flak for holding the meeting, at which they fired Boycott from the captaincy, so soon after the death of his mother. Geoffrey himself wasn't slow to make capital out of that either. The facts are that when the committee heard about Geoff's mother, Joe Lister rang him and offered to postpone the meeting to whatever date he felt able to attend. It was Geoffrey himself who said, 'No, don't bother. I'll be there.' At that time he didn't know he was going to get the chop – I doubt if the idea even entered his head. But when things went against Boycott at the meeting the Reform Group were quick to turn it around and use it to their own advantage, calling the committee all manner of names for not showing Boycott more consideration.

On top of that I still have in my possession, just in case the old memory is playing up after the best part of eight years, a copy of the notes I made to present to the members when they asked me for my views on the subject. I repeat, all I wanted was for the matter to be sorted out before my arrival, but it needed to be sorted on the basis of truth, and not on any fanciful evidence that may have been forthcoming. So my notes, typed in capital letters on a sheet of secretary Joe Lister's headed notepaper, started off like this:

> *I had spoken to quite a few of the players and therefore knew their feelings, but I then spoke to the players' representative and asked him what the feeling was regarding a change in captaincy. He assured me that when the players had discussed it, there was an overwhelming majority for a change. When the Reform Group disputed my letter I spoke to the representative again and asked him how the*

voting went. He told me that when the players were asked, not one player was in favour of Geoff Boycott remaining as captain.

Subsequently Geoff Boycott himself then contacted some of the players – but the question he asked them was not would they prefer him as captain but . . . would they play under him if he was captain. There is one heck of a difference – and the players answered that as members of the Yorkshire County Cricket team they would play under whoever was elected captain.

That was all the players could say; Boycott was trying to trap them into saying they would be happy to play under him – of course they would, they were professionals and they knew they would have to play under whichever captain they were given. But they didn't have to like it – and their vote had already made it clear they would be happier if that captain was not Geoff Boycott.

I also took the opportunity to reply to just two of the allegations that had been flying around, courtesy of members of the Reform Group. My notes read:

Finally, I would like to assure members that, contrary to Mr Sid Fielden's opinions, I am a man of integrity as anyone who knows me personally will tell you.

I would also like to make it very clear to Mr Mike Hellewell, who put up for the committee for the Barnsley area, that I am not a liar. My word has always been my bond and I would like to make it known here and now that I am not prepared to sit back any longer and have my name slandered.

Hellewell was a man I could never take to. But Sid Fielden intrigues me. It is well known that he finally abandoned the Reformers when he realized that, once they had assumed power in the elections early in 1984, they were

21

still interested in only one man – Geoffrey Boycott – and not in the interests of Yorkshire as a whole. Sometimes Fielden could be downright aggressive towards me, but at other times he did things that made me wonder. For instance, in July 1982, he sent me a short letter, neatly typed on his own personal, buff-coloured notepaper, saying simply: 'Dear Raymond. Just a brief note to let you know how much I have admired the way in which you have risen to the challenge in these past days. Wishing you all the best, etc., etc.'

That was shortly after I had taken the captaincy away from Chris Old in circumstances I will go into later, and led the team for a couple of games myself. Then I looked at the date at the top of Sid's letter . . . 10 July 1982 – the day on which I stood down from the side to play Gloucestershire at Bradford and asked Geoff Boycott to take over in my place. At that point I don't think Sid had changed too much!

I don't think I was naïve enough to believe that the winter of 1978–9, the last before I took over as manager at Heading-ley, would be allowed to slip peacefully by as I prepared myself for the tasks and tribulations that would lie ahead in April when I took up my appointment. That's how I would have liked it, of course. After all, the two top of the bill contestants for the following summer's title bout were well out of the way: Jack Hampshire, the new captain, was in Tasmania where he was playing for their Sheffield Shield side; and Geoff Boycott was on tour with England as Mike Brearley's men hammered the Australian Second XI, strip-ped of its stars by Kerry Packer's World Series circus, by five Tests to one.

Though there were several months and the whole winter ahead of me after leaving Leicestershire, I knew there was a big job to be done and a lot of work waiting. Shirley and I allowed ourselves a couple of breaks, amounting to about five weeks, in Spain, but they were the only relaxation we were going to have for quite a while. Then it was back to Yorkshire to attend a few meetings, renew old acquaint-ances and get stuck into raising some sponsorship to put the county on a sound financial footing for the bright and rosy future which, I hoped, stretched before us.

It was also a time to wind down the only other job I had ever had – selling Christmas cards, greetings cards and fireworks for a Leeds company called Shaun Wilson. I'd been doing that for the best part of twenty years. But now I knew I was going to have too much else on my plate. It had been OK in the past; if I had ever had to go away for a spell in the winter – like going on an England tour – I would rope in a couple of my mates like Barry Dudleston or John Steele at Leicester, to fill in for me while I was away. Up to now that had suited me. I was my own boss and I could work when I wanted to. Now all that had changed.

I soon found out that the only peace I was going to have during that winter came during the five weeks I spent in Spain . . . and I hadn't even started my job! I should have known. In the beginning it was only letters – some aimed at me and some at the committee. Some came direct to my house and some appeared in the columns of the Yorkshire papers – and right from the start it became obvious that my cardinal sin in the eyes of the Reformers was that letter I had sent to the committee asking them to sort out the Boycott business once and for all. I repeat that I didn't care which way the committee went; all I wanted was a decision one way or the other before I took over. But the letter-writers didn't seem interested in that – to them I had joined the Establishment. In their eyes Raymond Illingworth and the committee who had stripped Boycott of the captaincy were one and the same and both tarred with the same brush. Your average Yorkie, especially the pro-Boycott brigade, does rather tend to see things only in shades of black and white.

I was very definitely a distinct shade of black – especially to the Reform Group's star letter-writers like Tony Vann, Peter Briggs and Sid Fielden. Fielden, detective sergeant and lay preacher, was, of course, a familiar sight around Yorkshire cricket. I had known him for some time and I hear he's still around, having seen the follies of his earlier ways and switched sides. But Vann and Briggs were strangers and became known to me only by their signatures at the end of letters in the *Yorkshire Post* or *Evening Post*. I still haven't really met either of them, though there were times when I would have dearly loved to spend just a few minutes with them if only to give them a piece of my mind. Tony Vann, of course, finally rose to be chairman of the Reform Group's non-cricketing cricket committee which eventually fired me and which had no one who had any experience of playing cricket at first-class level, nor of administering a first-class county. I just wish Mr Vann could have been given half the hassle he dished out when his turn came to try and run the club.

The Reform Group's letter campaign began from the word 'go' though I must admit that the personal attacks on me and my family – the obscene phone calls and the anonymous letters – did not come until later. At this time I felt that the *Yorkshire Post*, which wields an immense influence on cricket in the county, could have served Yorkshire a lot better than they did. To be honest, I feel they have a lot to answer for.

The *YP*'s letters' column that winter used to come down about 5–1 in favour of Boycott and the Reformers. They could argue that five out of every six letters they received were anti-committee, but I do know of several members whose letters backing the committee never saw the light of day. Some of them even sent copies of those letters to me. I feel it was up to the *YP* to give a balanced and fair-minded view and that, in my opinion, is something they never did.

The journalists themselves, however, were much fairer. A lot of them took an anti-committee stand but they always tried to give a balanced view. John Callaghan, of the *Evening Post*, was quite open with me, saying that he was against a lot of the things the committee did but that he was not actually anti me. Quite often he wrote things in support of Boycott and that, by definition, were sometimes critical of me. But Cally was never personal.

Perhaps the least fair was Terry Brindle, of the *Yorkshire Post*, who has married an Australian girl and now lives in

Sydney. Yet I can sympathize with Terry. He was doing a lot of work with Geoffrey Boycott at the time, writing his books and ghosting articles for him. I'm sure that deep down Terry could laugh at Boycott and some of the things he used to say and do. But it was all right for him – he could go home and grin. He didn't get the letters and the abuse and the phone calls that I was receiving before the end.

So throughout the winter of 1978–9 the battle lines were being drawn. You could even go as far as to say the trenches were being dug in two theatres of war as far apart as England and Australia.

4

THE TEAM OR
THE MAN?

I was reading with ever-growing alarm the newspaper reports of the mounting tension between Jack Hampshire and
Geoff Boycott when their paths crossed 'Down Under'. The
inevitable crunch came at Hobart in the third week of the
Australian tour in January 1979, and you can bet your life
that, though I only had the papers to go on at the time, I made
it my business to find out as near as I could what took place.
The Yorkshire papers were a big help in this direction. They
had their own men out there and at a time like that, when
Yorkshire politics are being played out on the public stage,
they don't find it too hard to forget that this was an England
tour they were covering and concentrate on the really important goings-on . . . Yorkshire's!

I'm told there was a touch of the High Noons in Hobart that
day as the two Yorkie gunslingers hit town. They passed
each other in the pavilion without speaking, they sat within
a couple of places of each other at lunch without saying a
word. Boycott, stationed at mid off, turned his back as
Hampshire walked past him on his way to the wicket for his
first innings and must have been immeasurably cheered
when Chris Old (Chilly) had his new captain caught behind
for nought.

England vice captain Bob Willis declared his first innings
with Boycott 90 not out in a total of 210 and finally gave full
rein to his impish sense of humour by allowing Geoffrey to
bowl the final over of a meaningless match to Hampshire.

I'm told that Hamps did make at least one visit to the England team hotel – but it wasn't to make the peace. Boycott did not even appear. Hamps had to be content with a drink with David Bairstow (Bluey) and Chris Old and his peace-making was forced to wait until Tasmania, as luck would have it, won the Gillette Cup and with it the right to meet the tourists again, in a challenge match at Melbourne early in February.

Geoffrey was in the nets – where else? – when Hamps strolled across and asked him how he was. 'I'm OK. How are you?' replied Boycs and the ice was broken – or at least cracked. Hampshire then bowled a few gentle deliveries to Boycs and went away thinking the ice was really melting. But with Geoffrey it's never quite as easy as that.

I had known Boycott since he first joined Yorkshire in 1961. And I was worried. It didn't look to me as if Geoffrey had made any real effort in Tasmania to go even half-way towards meeting Jack Hampshire, yet it had been a Heaven-sent opportunity to put their relationship on a sound and sensible footing for the coming season.

Geoffrey can be so evasive when anything crops up that he doesn't want to discuss. Even when you know he's up to something – like little chats in the corner of the dressing room with one or two of his cronies, or meetings round the back of the pavilion with members of the Reform Group – he's so careful not to do anything you can actually put your finger on that you can end up wondering if you're half-way round the bend.

So I knew Geoffrey would never be downright rebellious to Jack Hampshire. But I also had a fair idea that he wouldn't go out of his way to help either – not unless he thought there was something in it for him. The same thing happened when Chris Old became captain two years later and Hamps finally decided – on the day his wife was openly insulted in a local supermarket – that Yorkshire was no longer the place for him and made tracks across the county border to Derbyshire.

The problem is that you never really know what Boycott is

thinking – it's just that there is always an atmosphere, especially in the dressing room, when he is around. You can have all the players together in pre-season training and everything will be going well – laughter, jokes, little pranks, just like the old days. Then Geoffrey will return from an England tour, come back to Yorkshire, and everything changes.

In many ways I have a lot of sympathy for Geoffrey, though. It couldn't have been easy for him having to deal with the Yorkshire committee in the eight years he was captain and I've no doubt that drove him further into his shell and made him even more introverted. But there was no getting away from the fact that the first character trait you would apply to Geoffrey would be 'selfish'.

His batting was almost always selfish and I must say I feel that his attitude towards Jack Hampshire came under the same heading. Hamps was an honest and open lad. He would speak his mind if he had anything to say and then sit down and have a pint with you afterwards. He had given Boycott loyal service in the eight years that Geoffrey was captain and I felt the least he could expect was loyalty in return.

But the feeling was growing as the summer of 1979 wore on that Boycott would not be too unhappy if Yorkshire failed to win anything in their first year without him at the helm. His lady friend, Ann Wyatt, was once overheard saying as much. But again, I could never pin anything like that directly at Geoffrey's door. He was too canny for that.

At least I knew he would always bat as well as he could – his pride wouldn't allow him to do otherwise. There's never any problem with him in that direction – he's too much of a professional. He would never sulk in the field either – again he knew that would reflect badly on him as a professional cricketer. He would always be there on time, smartly turned out and remarkably fit for a man of his age, who, by that summer of 1979, was fast approaching forty.

It was typical of Geoffrey that he should finish top of Yorkshire's batting that summer with a staggering average of 116. But figures don't prove everything, and by now I was starting to look at just how and when Geoffrey made his runs and of what real value they were to his side. I still hadn't forgotten his little drama of despair when he ran out Derek Randall on his Test comeback in 1977.

Basically, Geoffrey was very insecure. He was petrified of failure and from the very first day he arrived in the Yorkshire dressing room he would pester the older players with questions like: 'Do you really think I'm a good player?' They would tell him: 'Of course you are. Now get out there and prove it.' The trouble with Geoff was that, even when he himself was a senior, with a string of Test matches behind him, he could never bring himself to give that same sort of encouragement to the youngsters under him. He was still too busy looking for it himself.

But why? He was on the way to making more Test runs than any Englishman before and more than any other player except Sunil Gavaskar. Yet he still needed his ego boosted and he still wanted to be told what to do when he was in the middle. We had to spell it out to him stage by stage: 'Look, Geoff, we need 30 runs off the next 10 overs' – things like that. Of course, a player of his experience knew darned well what was wanted but he needed to be told so he would then have an excuse for making only 30 runs off the next 10 overs and not, perhaps, 31 or 32. We knew that, having said 30, that was what we would get – 29 or 30 . . . but not 31. Then he could pace himself and not have to take any risks like trying to hit over the top.

He was always looking for an excuse to go on batting in his own way at his own pace. Demanding to be given a target by his captain was one way of making sure that somebody else drew up the rules and, knowing nobody would ask the impossible of him, Geoffrey was happy to see they were given what they wanted – and never one jot more. It also suited him to let both his team mates and the rest of the world know that, in his opinion, he was the only competent player in the side . . . something that had already landed him in trouble with the Yorkshire committee. Trouble or not, that view gave Geoffrey a marvellous excuse to bat exactly the way he wanted – slowly. If enough people began to believe he was the only worthwhile player in the team they would eventually start to believe the very thing he wanted – that if he got out, all was lost.

Yet Boycott wasn't the only good player in the Yorkshire dressing room – let alone in the England one. And it is also why I say, without any doubt, that Geoffrey Boycott, despite all his runs and records, was *not* a great batsman. A good one, yes. But not a great one. Yet the tragedy is that Geoffrey could have been a great batsman if only he had taken a risk just once or twice . . . if only he had been under a captain throughout his career who had the power to make him get a move on – or else! That was what Brian Close did when Boycott hit that marvellous 146 in the Gillette Cup Final against Surrey in 1965.

The Reform Group were very fond of quoting Geoffrey's batting figures to back up their arguments, but I would ask them to check on how many matches he had actually *won* for Yorkshire. He has saved some, of course. Batting out the last day for a nice little 100 not out and nobody to find fault with it is exactly his idea of heaven. But on a good wicket he would take so long to make his runs you needed to have the best bowling side in the world to be sure of getting the others out in the remaining time. The only situation I can think of where Geoffrey could actually win you a game would be on an indifferent pitch where you needed 200 or so to win. He could then drop anchor at one end and make 80 or 90 while the others would pick up the rest between them.

He was so orthodox he would let you bowl to him. If you knew where you were going to pitch it, you knew where Geoffrey was going to hit it – it was too much of a risk for him to try something different, to try and make things up a little as he went along. A great player is always prepared to take the bowlers on and show them who is boss, but Geoff never did. You could bowl spinners at him, especially in his earlier days, and as long as you kept them up and bowled straight he would never make a run. And teams soon rumbled him – set

an orthodox field with a ring saving the singles and Geoff
would struggle, because he was never prepared to have a
dart.

In many ways I would liken Boycott to Colin Cowdrey.
Both were very, very good defensive players, but they never
really dominated. Now put Peter May in a similar situation
and he would take control. Boycott and Cowdrey would let
people bowl to them, but if you didn't bowl well to Peter May
he would win you out, take you apart. That is true greatness: the ability to produce a century in two-and-a-half hours
and go on to 150 in the next half hour or so – and to do it
regularly.

Having aired my views on Boycott as a player and a man
quite openly and, I hope, fairly, it gave my ego quite a boost
when I read what was said about him when Yorkshire finally
took the bull by the horns and fired him at the end of last
season. Shirley and I were already in Torremolinos for our
winter break when the news came through that Geoffrey,
coming up to his forty-sixth birthday, was not being retained
for 1987.

This time there were no rows and no dissenting voices, not
like three years earlier when Yorkshire had also tried to be
rid of him. And this time, on 23 September 1986, some of the
big names, like Brian Close, chairman of the Yorkshire
cricket sub-committee, came right out and talked of the
problems they had had in the dressing room with Geoffrey.
At last Close admitted that Boycott was selfish – something I
had been trying to tell them for years. For official consump-
tion Close told the world: 'The good of Yorkshire cricket
came first. I would have loved Boycott to go on making runs
and breaking records. But in reality his retention would not
have helped us.'

What it boiled down to was that Boycott, with his position
as an elected member of the committee, was making life
unbearable for many of the other players. The club had given
him the chance to resign, either as a committee member, or
as a player. As time went on it became increasingly obvious

that Geoffrey was not going to take advantage of their offer, and something had to be done.

The pressures that led Yorkshire to do that 'something' came out pretty clearly when Close told the *Sun*'s Ian Todd: 'Geoff Boycott may have been a great success in recent years, but Yorkshire cricket has been anything but. If Geoff had resigned from the committee last summer and thrown in his lot with the rest of the players, we would probably have offered him another contract. But he refused. It was his way of putting himself first just as he always has throughout his career. That's why he had to go for the sake of Yorkshire cricket.'

The previous winter the club had passed a resolution to prevent a current player ever becoming a committee member again. 'That resolution was Boycott's cue to step down a year before it came into effect, but that's not his way,' said Close. 'He didn't want to become just another player again.'

The fact that the Reform Group finally accepted Boycott's sacking came as no surprise to me. Tony Vann, a committee man himself, said, 'I'm stunned by the decision, but I have to accept it with good grace because that's democracy.' It's a great pity he and some of his pals hadn't learned about democracy during 1979–83 when they were making my life hell.

Luckily I was in Spain when all this happened – but regular visits to the newspaper stall in Torremolinos kept me in touch, even if they did have the English papers a day late. I soon saw that Geoffrey had sold his story to the *Daily Mail* and was promising that his twenty-four-year-old collection of newspaper cuttings, diaries, notes of conversations and tapes would all appear in a book in the summer of 1987. I noticed, without undue surprise, that Geoffrey has already told the *Daily Mail* that he rated me as a fine captain, but no great shakes as a manager. I wonder if the book will also expose me as one of the 'handful of prejudiced men he failed to convince of the difference between self-discipline, single-mindedness and mere selfishness'. Roll on summer . . . I can hardly wait!

Ray Illingworth

This time eight years ago, however, there were other things on my mind. We were approaching the 1979 season – my first as manager of Yorkshire, and Jack Hampshire's first as captain. It was being hailed – in some quarters, anyway – as the start of a new era of Yorkshire cricket . . . the chance to recapture the glory of the past. So how did 1979 turn out?

5

NO BALL

There was only one major bust-up that summer, plus an outbreak of no balling that hit our bowlers like a plague of German measles, but the undercurrent of bad feeling and sniping was always so obvious that both Shirley and I reached the end of that season – our first, mind you – wishing we had not made the move back to Yorkshire. We had taken quite a long time before arriving at our decision to return. We knew the problems Yorkshire had been experiencing, even before I got back, but we had the education of our two daughters to think of – and Shirley, despite her doubts, has never been one of those wives who tries to influence her husband. She will stand by me in whatever I think is best for us. Yet by the end of 1979 she was saying, 'The day you come home and tell me you've packed it in will be the happiest day of my life.' Neither of us had expected it to be a bed of roses, but equally neither of us had realized just how unpleasant it was going to be.

Even the players were being drawn into the disputes and that made me angry; they were my first responsibility and I wanted to make sure they were in the right frame of mind to play cricket. But they knew what was going on – right from the start. They would look out of the dressing room window and spot a member or two of the Reform Group slipping into the ground and say, 'Hello, the Mafia's here again.' We didn't do all that great in 1979, but it was amazing we did anything at all.

What we did do was to reach the semifinals of the Benson &
Hedges Cup, when we lost rather controversially to Essex at
Chelmsford; the quarter-finals of the Gillette Cup, as it was
still called; a slight rise in the John Player League; and
seventh position in the Championship – even if that was
three places down on the previous year, it was still not bad.
And all of that could have been a lot better but for those no
balls, some 350 of them in the county Championship and so
many in one-day competitions that we were regularly giving
our opponents at least two overs more than we were facing.
It's amazing we did as well as we did.

It has always annoyed me to see some England bowlers in
the nets – bowling off seventeen or eighteen yards without a
care in the world – and then wondering why they can't get it
right when the chips are down out there in the middle. I
know some of them think that nets are for batsmen, not
bowlers. Even if that is so – and I don't subscribe to that
theory – why don't the bowlers try to give their batsmen
something like the real thing in the nets? It seems good
enough for the West Indies fast bowlers, so on that basis I
asked Clive Lloyd, their captain, how he managed to handle
them. But though he has anything up to four or five fast
bowlers at the one time, Clive still wasn't able to suggest
anything I hadn't been trying already.

Unfortunately, some of the Yorkshire bowlers soon
showed that summer that getting it right in the nets was
only half the battle, if that. When you move out to the
middle things like nerves, tension and excitement take over
– and nobody suffered more than Arnie Sidebottom. I would
have thought that Arnie, with all his experience of playing
soccer in front of big crowds during his days with Manchester
United, would have been able to overcome all that. Not at all.

I used to spend hours with Arnie. In the nets I would stand
as umpire and watch every ball he bowled – and if his front
foot strayed I would call him, and keep on until he got it
right. Before a match we would go out into the middle and
mark out his run exactly so we were both satisfied it was
correct. And we would do that at both ends, so it didn't matter

which way Arnie had to bowl – we knew his run-up would be correctly marked. Then he would come on for his first over and in no time at all the umpire was sticking out his arm and shouting 'No ball!' Oh, Arnie!

My most bitter regret about that first season was that we didn't win our Benson & Hedges semifinal against Essex and the events that brought about our defeat. I am certain that if we had beaten Essex and gone on to Lord's, we had it in us to beat Surrey, the other finalists, and so win a trophy in my first season as manager. How often I sit and wonder what a difference that would have made to the course of Yorkshire cricket.

The match at Chelmsford took place on 4 July, but the scene was set at Harrogate three days earlier. Geoff Boycott and Richard Lumb cashed in on a pretty flat track to put on 288 for the first wicket against Somerset – Geoffrey's share being 130 not out. But he damaged a hamstring during the course of that innings and, though he didn't come off at the time, he was unable to bat in the second innings.

We drove down to Chelmsford on the Tuesday and early the next morning I put on my track suit and said to Geoffrey, 'Come on, let's jog round the ground and see how your leg is.' He said, 'I can't run at all.' I said, 'You can't even jog?' And he said, 'No, I can't even go steady.' That was it as far as I was concerned. You can't take a half-fit player into a vital one-day match and I said, 'In that case there's no decision to make. You obviously can't play.' He had, in effect, ruled himself out of the game by saying he couldn't even jog. He had even told Jack Hampshire. Yet he went to the press and told them I had left him out of the match – dropped him. I can tell you I was bloody annoyed, and so was Hampshire. It was by his own admission that Boycott was unfit; if he had been fit he would most certainly have played and almost equally as certainly it would have only needed a typically steady, professional knock from him for us to have won the tie and gone on to Lord's.

A victory there could have opened all sorts of doors to us, just as it did at Leicester when we won the Benson & Hedges

Cup in 1972. As it was, we had to play three youngsters, Kevin Sharp, Bill Athey and Jim Love, at numbers three, four and five and they managed only three runs between them after Jack Hampshire, promoted to open in Boycott's place, had helped Lumb to get us away with a first wicket stand of 107. All we needed was somebody to bat sensibly. He didn't have to go mad as a score of 200 or so would have been enough in difficult conditions. In the end we made only 173–9 in our 55 overs. We made Essex work for them, but they had the best of the conditions and won by three wickets with an over to spare. I had learned at Leicester that once you have won a one-day cup the confidence seems to rub off and everyone believes in themselves. With that little bit of belief I think we could have come near to winning the Championship in 1979 – but it all fell down that July day at Chelmsford.

By the end of 1980 I was starting to feel that at last we were making some progress. It was not a bad season for Yorkshire, especially as we finished sixth in the county Championship and, but for an almost complete wash-out on the last day of our last home match against Derbyshire at Scarborough, would almost certainly have ended up fourth. The one cloud on the horizon for me was that at the end of the season Jack Hampshire, our captain, decided he had had enough of the backbiting and insults of the Reform Group and called it a day, giving up the captaincy and, a year later, finally leaving Yorkshire altogether and going to Derbyshire.

The Reform Group and their allies had no idea the harm they were doing to Yorkshire and the hounding of Jack Hampshire, culminating in a harrowing verbal assault on his wife, Judy, lost the county an experienced, talented and loyal player at the very time that he was needed the most. If I had to be critical of Hamps I would have to be honest and say that he did not have a lot of flair as a captain, particularly in his use of spinners, and if he had shown just a little more imagination in that department we might have finished in the top three in 1980.

But he had taken the job on when many others were not prepared to risk it – and there wasn't much he could have done about the last match. Geoffrey Boycott gave us the platform with the highest score of the season – 154 not out in our total of 338–6 declared. Chris Old took 4–34 to bowl Derbyshire out for 136 and they were soon in trouble again when they were asked to follow on. But on the last day, despite frantic mopping-up operations with everything we could lay our hands on, we managed only 9 overs late in the day and Derbyshire wriggled out at 180 – another 3 wickets and another 12 points and we would have been fourth, only 3 points behind third-placed Notts.

But if that came as a blow, it was nothing to the sickness I felt inside when Wisden's account of the season gave their opinion that many of Yorkshire's problems had not been solved by my appointment as manager, 'partly because no real discipline has been imposed'. It was another triumph for the Reform Group; by following us around, by spying on the players and picking up every slight fault they could find and then bombarding the Yorkshire papers with letters every couple of minutes, they'd built up an atmosphere where people were starting to fall for their propaganda.

So I'm going to bash those lies on the head right now. I can claim – and I defy anyone to show otherwise – that I have never been involved with any side, either as manager or captain, where discipline has been bad. If you don't believe me, have a word with Maurice Fenner, who was the Kent secretary until a couple of years ago. Mr Fenner, at the request of the Kent members, wrote not one, but two letters to Yorkshire congratulating us on the smart appearance and good behaviour of our players when we played at Canterbury. And it wasn't only Kent – quite a number of other counties took the trouble to write and tell us we were the smartest side they had seen on their grounds.

You don't receive compliments like that by luck. One of the first things I did as manager was to have uniforms made – light blue suits with the White Rose of Yorkshire on the breast pocket. The players had to wear either them or a blazer, with tie, for the first two days of any Championship match with the option of wearing travelling gear for the final day, and even that had to be what I call 'smart casual' – no jeans or cords, just tidy golf gear. It had to be jacket and tie for one-day games as well, unless they were playing away and were travelling on the same day. In that event they were allowed to go in their 'smart casual' gear.

If there were any complaints flying about, they certainly weren't coming from the players. To a man, I had them believing, as I believe, that if they took a pride in playing for Yorkshire, they would also take pride in the way they represented Yorkshire – on and off the field. That's why you never saw a player of mine going on the field looking as if he'd just crawled out of bed. If your appearance is scruffy, then your performance will match. But if you can go out there looking like a cricketer, then you're much more likely to play like one. Ask Geoffrey Boycott!

I reached the end of the 1981 season – my third as manager and Chris Old's first as captain – with mixed feelings. On the playing side I could see signs of better days ahead; all we needed was a bit of luck. But on the political front . . . oh dear! The rows, or misunderstandings if you prefer, seemed to be happening more often and were becoming more public and more bitter.

Things were getting to such a pitch that the notes I prepared at the end of the season as the basis of my report to the committee now ran into four closely typed foolscap pages. And I found myself being forced to leave the playing side of the club's affairs until last, even though that was what I had once believed I had been brought back to Yorkshire to handle.

The Reform Group's campaign to have me fired hotted up and the county committee felt it necessary to institute an 'in-depth investigation' into all the club's affairs. The record books will show that we slipped from sixth to tenth in the Championship, but what they will not show is some of the reasons for that.

No Ball

This is what my report to the committee said:

> *In the Championship we had a very wet start to the season, and when we batted well – making almost 400 at Warwickshire and 348–9 against Lancashire at Old Trafford, the rain came and ruined both games. If we could have got off to a good start it could have made a bit of difference, but to be honest we had such a run of injuries it is doubtful if anything could have helped. In fact, the first Championship match for which I selected from all our capped players was at Chesterfield at the end of August, and we won that by six wickets. For the record, we suffered eight fractures, plus serious injuries to Sidebottom, Dennis, Johnson, Ramage, Old, Athey, Sharp, Stevenson and Hartley.*

Our physio's room, which, as a matter of fact, was one of the first improvements I made at Headingley when I took over in 1979, really earned its money in 1981 – at times you would have thought we were a Rugby League club, not a cricket team!

At the end of my report I also mentioned one of those things that everyone in cricket knows about but few people, with the possible exception of the occasional beaten captain, ever talks about – prepared pitches. My report read: 'One thing that has been proved this season is the fact that if you want to do anything in the Championship you must play on wickets for your home matches that (1) produce finishes, and (2) help the type of attack which your side possesses. There is no doubt that Notts, Sussex, Essex and Somerset have done this.'

The season got off to a fairly good start when we qualified for the Benson & Hedges quarter-finals by finishing at the top of a fairly strong group. We then lost a good match against Somerset, one of the best one-day teams in the country, by 3 wickets at Headingley after we had made

221–9 – not a bad performance, especially as Somerset eventually went on to beat Surrey in the final at Lord's.

And this is what my report said about the John Player League – some of the remarks I made about bringing in the youngsters take on a deeper significance as the story unfolds.

> *The Sunday League was terribly affected, for us anyway, by the weather, so at the half-way stage of the season I decided to play the youngsters. The effect was dramatic, for team spirit improved tremendously with everyone playing for each other and four out of the next five games were won against some very good sides, including Somerset, Hampshire, Northants and Derbyshire, three of whom reached one-day finals at Lord's that season.*

I went on to report that the improvement in team spirit continued with us winning the Fenner Trophy at Scarborough, beating Essex, one of the best limited-overs teams in the land, in the final. And, I must emphasize, there was no arrangement for the prize money to be split, come what may. Both teams were playing for keeps!

At this point I had to make, sadly, these comments: 'I mention team spirit because I felt that having G. Boycott in the side was detrimental to team spirit. I have given the management committee details of incidents during the season which I felt were detrimental to harmony.'

One of those incidents, in a long season packed with them, saw the end of our hopes in the NatWest Trophy when we lost by 6 wickets to Kent at Canterbury in the first round on 11 July. Kent are never an easy team to beat, especially in front of their own crowd and Derek Underwood (Deadly) is never an easy bowler to get away. But on this occasion Deadly was allowed to bowl his 12 overs for 10 runs and Boycott, who should have been well set by then, batted throughout his spell. I told Geoffrey in no uncertain terms that he should have got on or got out – but that's not his way. It was left to John Hampshire and David Bairstow, who came together at

144–5 with 11 overs remaining, to rattle us up to 222–6. But it was still not enough and Kent won with sixteen balls to spare.

Yet one of Boycott's main grouses was that I didn't pick him for Sunday League games. He thought his bowling would be useful in the John Player League and I have little doubt he was right, but he used to take that further and refuse to bowl in the three-day matches . . . and with our crop of injuries he could have been really useful on occasions. Arnie Sidebottom and Chris Old, our regular opening bowlers, managed fewer than 700 overs between them in the Championship and situations developed, like the one at Chesterfield in August, where Boycott's mean little inswingers would have been very handy. In that game Derbyshire made 400 in their first innings and, though we eventually won a declaration match by 6 wickets, we could have done with a few overs from Boycott while John Wright was racing to 150 in their first innings. But he refused to bowl.

I wished things could have been different; after all, I had nothing against Geoffrey personally, except for the influence he was having on the rest of the team. When we were both just players together I got on with him better than most people – we thought about the game in the same way and we respected each other's cricket ability. But, sadly, my report at the end of 1981 ended with these words:

> *Finally, gentlemen, I would just like to say that you brought me back to Yorkshire to do a job. I believe I can do that job and if you talk to anyone connected with cricket in this country I believe 90 per cent of them would agree. But there is no way we can ever get a team spirit all the while Geoffrey Boycott is playing for Yorkshire.*
>
> *It is like a cloud descending on the dressing room when he comes back from Test matches and team spirit is the most important thing a Yorkshire side can have. Chris Old, I am sure, will verify this statement. As somebody said at a recent dinner, we*

*have a weed in the garden which must be removed to
let the roses bloom.*

I assume he meant the White Roses!

In case anyone feels I am being a bit hard on Geoffrey, it is worth going back again on one incident that soured the season of 1981.

Chris Old, as I have said, was captain for 1981 and he felt he would be able to get on OK with Boycs – we had had a chat in Barbados when I was out in the West Indies watching the Test. I'm afraid I didn't share Old's optimism, but I was glad to hear he was using the tour for a chance to speak to Boycott and establish a few ground rules for the coming season. Unfortunately they weren't kept for very long – no longer than 27 May when we played Kent at Dartford. Boycott and David Bairstow turned up early at the ground, saw that it was raining, and decided play could not start until lunch at the earliest. Unfortunately it was not their decision to make and the umpires thought otherwise, deciding that a morning start, though delayed, was possible. Eventually they appeared in time to take the field with the rest of the lads, but I was still angry they had not been there at the scheduled starting time – that was their job and it was not up to them to decide when the game might or might not start, no matter what the weather was like. Bairstow took my reprimand in a good-enough spirit and so, I thought, did Boycott. Until Chris Old went up to him some time later in the day to ask him, not surprisingly, since it was his first month as captain, for some advice. Boycott told him, 'It's nothing to do with me. You're the captain – get on with it.' I'm afraid Chris Old's illusions of friendship and peace had not lasted very long.

6

A QUESTION OF
CAPTAINS

Scarborough, that windy little town on the east coast of Yorkshire, is a place most people go to for a holiday – a complete rest by the sea, you might say. But it was far from that for me as it cropped up again and again during that hectic summer of 1981. For Scarborough was where I first made Neil Hartley, only twenty-five, uncapped and largely unproven, captain of Yorkshire for the first time, and Scarborough it was where he skippered us in the John Player League – and won against Somerset. It was Scarborough where I had a row with David Bairstow (Bluey), who thought he ought to have been made captain in Chris Old's absence – and it was Scarborough where I had to ban Geoff Boycott after his outburst against me in a bookshop in York. I like Scarborough . . . it's bracing, lively, friendly. But by September 1981 I was starting to wish I had never heard of it!

The first hint of trouble came when I made Neil Hartley captain for the Championship match against Warwickshire on 29 July 1981 when Chris Old was injured and Geoff Boycott was at Edgbaston for the fourth Test against Australia. A few days later he skippered us against Somerset in the John Player League and we beat them, Viv Richards, Joel Garner and all, by 20 runs.

We didn't have a vice captain then because in the past, one or two players had filled that role and then we found they were not good enough to command a place in the side. Obviously a lot of people objected to having an uncapped

45

player as captain and the Reform Group, unable to keep out of anything, threw their weight in behind David Bairstow, who also felt strongly that he should have been given the job. That led to my famous row with Bluey in the bar of the Royal Hotel at Scarborough which I shall talk about later. But nothing happened to make me sorry I had plumped for Hartley, even though I believe, if my memory serves me right, that he was the first and only uncapped player ever to lead Yorkshire. He was the right man for the job and he should be captain of Yorkshire right now.

I know the gossips said I only gave Neil the job because he was going out with my daughter Vicky, so I'd like to hit that one on the head right now. First of all, Neil and Vicky had split up twelve months before I made him captain. People said Neil was married, but he had been separated a good twelve months when he met Vicky. And another thing – if he had still been seeing Vicky it would have made me go the other way. I would have been less likely to give him the job, not more so.

It's amazing how rumour and gossip sticks; Vicky and Peter, her husband, were watching a match at Headingley only last season when they heard a man in front of them point towards Neil and say, 'That's young Hartley! He's married to Illy's daughter, you know.' It's a good job they were able to see the funny side of it.

Neil had always been my choice for captain, ever since he did the twelfth man duties a few times as a youngster and we used to sit and talk about captaincy. He was captain of Bingley in the Bradford League when he was only nineteen and he led them to the Priestley Cup and league double. With eight O Levels and three A Levels he was a bright lad, too. I knew his thinking on the game was similar to my own and I used to ask him, 'What would you do in this situation?' or 'What bowler would you have on now?' He was tactically very aware – he knew when to bowl the spinners, when to put on the seamers and how to use them. And he was keen on talking and learning more about the game.

We needed somebody with a bit of flair and Hartley had

more upstairs than anybody else on the staff. I did discuss the appointment with one or two people whose opinions I respected, but deep down I knew it was the right decision, so I went ahead and did it. I am only sorry that Yorkshire did not take their chance and offer Neil the captaincy again in 1984 when the opportunity arose. I am sure that 90 per cent of the committee wanted Hartley at the end of 1983 when they decided not to offer Geoff Boycott another contract – a decision smartly overturned when the Reformers came to power early in 1984. But in 1983 the committee felt their removal of Boycott would be sweetened in the eyes of the public if they gave the captaincy to David Bairstow – an enthusiastic and loyal Tyke, but never a captain as long as he breathes. Once again the committee did not have the guts to do the right thing and the club are still paying for it. Hartley may never become captain now and for three years the club were stuck with Bairstow, who has now given way to Phil Carrick.

The only objections anyone could come up with against Hartley was that he might, and only might, not be quite a good enough player. But I don't agree. He would average around 25 with the bat and was the fittest man on the staff. Not for nothing did the players nickname Neil 'Hare' and he would save you 10 or 15 runs in the field, as well as being able to bowl a few useful overs with his little seamers.

His fitness and his enthusiasm meant Neil could be relied upon to bring the best out of the others – like the way he coached and trained Simon Dennis while they were in South Africa together. He did it so well that in 1983 Simon bowled 525 overs for us compared to 66 the year before.

Neil had been an amateur soccer player with Bradford City for five years before breaking a leg and he also played Rugby Union with Bingley. The confidence rugby and soccer gave him helped him to handle the other players – and there were times when he needed it. He was always quiet and firm – there's no other way for a good skipper. He had everything against him; obviously he was only captain because a number of senior players were absent and that made the side that much weaker to start with. There was also a fair amount of resentment, but Neil was never afraid to do what he knew to be right. He was strong when he had to be and it couldn't have been easy for an uncapped player to go up to a senior bowler – one like Graham Stevenson, who had played for England – and tell him he wasn't doing it right or the way he wanted. He had to put up with some aggro from Stevo, but it made it all worthwhile at the end of the season when Arnie Sidebottom came to me and said, 'I'll tell you this straight. I was against Neil at the start, but if he's captain next year I'll be behind him 100 per cent.'

Neil, you see, never had to shout and bawl or wave his arms about. Good skippers don't. That's where Bairstow goes wrong; people on the edge hear him shouting and yelling and they think he's a good skipper, but good captains don't do that. All you should have to do is move an arm or give a little nod and people should be watching you and be aware of what's going on. If anyone causes me to shout or bawl I'll give him such a rollicking in the dressing room he'll never do it again. It happened once in all the time I was at Leicester – and it never happened again. And why should it? Most county sides field well, you've got four good bowlers and the rest should pretty well take care of itself. There will be the odd day when somebody like Viv Richards or Ian Botham takes you apart for an hour or so, but if you stick to basics it won't happen very often.

I'm not trying to knock Bairstow. Bluey is a Yorkie through and through and he would give his life for the club. It's just that I feel Neil Hartley would have made a far better captain and I have no doubt any Yorkshire player would tell you the same. I really think the county stuck with Bairstow for so long simply because they landed themselves in a situation where they didn't want any more changes. There'd been that much coming and going that all they wanted was a period of peace and tranquillity and Bluey gave it to them. But deep down he'll always be what he is – a trusty Sergeant Major but never an officer!

It's not Bluey's fault he's a wicket-keeper either – but there's no getting away from the fact that it's the hardest job in the world to be a wicket-keeper and a captain. It's untidy, and I like tidy cricket. Very few people have ever managed to combine the two jobs successfully, and that is one of the reasons that Yorkshire's over rates have been so slow in recent seasons. A wicket-keeper can be very useful for giving advice to his captain as he sees most of what is going on, but if he has to try and convey that information directly to his bowlers he can find himself making treks of up to forty yards every few balls. And a wicket-keeper can't find time to think ahead and plan in the way that a captain must – he has enough on his plate concentrating on what is going on in the present.

Bairstow wanted the job – no doubt about that – and I might have thought less of him if he hadn't. I can understand him being upset when I gave it to Neil Hartley. Bairstow was undoubtedly the senior player in the side that played Warwickshire – Neil's first game as skipper.

Incidentally, Neil Hartley's promotion wasn't the only experiment I made at that time. It was against Warwickshire that I gave a first senior game to a young seam bowler from Sheffield named Steve Stuchbury – only to find that the club, probably through secretary Joe Lister, had forgotten to register him! It wasn't only on the field that Yorkshire were making a mess of things. Apart from David Ryder, the assistant secretary, who was always the one I went to if I wanted anything done, the back-room boys weren't too hot, either.

The trouble with Bluey is that his emotions are a bit too near the surface at times. And that's definitely how it was that night at the Royal Hotel, especially as he was fired up with a few drinks as well. He walked straight up to me in a fairly crowded bar and came right out with it – he wanted to be captain and told me so in no uncertain terms. I explained one or two of the reasons I had chosen Hartley and then said I didn't think a crowded bar was the place to be carrying on a discussion about it. I told him we would talk quietly and sensibly at another time and in another place.

Scarborough was full of Yorkshire supporters and a good

many of them were in that bar at the Royal. I didn't want any rumours of a row getting out, but it was too late. A local freelance reporter named Martin Searby was in the bar and next day it was in the papers and on the radio. Even the Reform Group seemed to have been given a fairly detailed briefing. Searby later denied that he had been listening to the conversation between me and Bluey – he said the barman had told him all about it. So I said to Searby, 'A crowded bar in the bloody Royal, we're right down one end and the barman's running up and down like a blue-arsed fly trying to serve a dozen people all at once and he's still got time to listen in detail to what we're saying. Come off it!' The footnote is typical Bluey – and good luck to him. He went out the next day and kept wicket as well as ever he could when Warwickshire batted; then he hit a top score of 62 in our only innings as the match petered out in a draw because we just didn't have the bowling to make the most of our first innings lead of 96.

The next notable occurrence of 1981 may seem a commonplace little event – nothing more than a run out, the sort of thing that happens all the time. But this sort of run out was happening far too often, for it involved Geoffrey Boycott. And this one, like a number of other incidents, led to Yorkshire losing one of their most promising and talented young players – a batsman who ended up playing for England and was on the 1986–7 tour of Australia: Bill Athey. He didn't leave Yorkshire until 1983, but it was an incident in the Championship match against Hampshire in the second week of August 1981 that told young Bill his days as a Tyke were numbered.

We had been having problems all season. Not only were Athey and Boycott losing us up to 10 or 15 singles in every one-day match by their mutual mistrust of each other, but they were also costing us wickets. So one day at Leeds I got them together and spelled it out. 'Look,' I said. 'We've got to build some confidence. If the ball's hit between cover and mid-wicket the striker's got to call and the other batsman's got to be looking at him and going on his call. If it goes behind square leg or down to third man, the running batsman's got to call and the striker has to go on his call. We've got to have the confidence to do this.'

Happy that I had given them both a good going over, I sent them out for the next match, which was the one against Hampshire at Middlesbrough. It happened to be where Bill Athey's father had played league cricket for twenty-five years and where he had been president since 1975. A pity then that in the second innings, after he had made 8, Bill was run out by Boycott by a good two or three yards – stuffed out of sight, as they say in the game. Little did it please Bill that later in the same innings Boycott was also run out; he still stormed into the dressing room, hurled his bat against the wall in time-honoured fashion, and declared, 'Well, that's it!' What could I say? I'd done all I could, I'd got them together – and straightaway one of them is run out.

I knew what Bill was saying. From that moment on it was each man for himself and Bill made sure he was never run out again. He watched every ball, wherever it went, and only ran when he felt it was safe to do so – in fact, I think he even did Boycs a couple of times. But I felt it was a pity; every batsman makes a mistake now and then and runs out his partner. It's all part of the game. It's a rotten way to be out, but it's something you just have to learn to accept. What rankled with Athey, and with others, was that with Boycott it happened far too often – and he was very rarely the one who had to go. He was a bad judge of a run, but whereas most players, having seen they'd made a mistake, would sacrifice themselves, it seems that Boycott always made sure he was the one to survive, very often pushing the other man into running. It wasn't very nice.

7

SCARBOROUGH
AND SUSPENSION

The biggest bust-up of 1981 came, of course, at the beginning of September, when I had to suspend Geoffrey Boycott for remarks I heard he had made about me at a book-signing session in W. H. Smith in York. Here he made his now notorious outburst that he was going to seek a showdown with me – a speech that somebody had made sure would be well covered by local television and radio. At the time it looked like yet another ill-considered outburst from our rather volatile opening batsman, although it did seem odd that a television camera had been there to record it. But as time went on, as more events unfurled and more people came forward to tell me what they knew and had heard, it all took on the appearance of a well-orchestrated plot by the Reform Group. Geoffrey was probably more of a pawn in rather than the brain behind their plans to discredit me and so have me removed from my job as Yorkshire's manager.

The notes I made before making my report to the committee at the end of the 1981 season bear out the way I was thinking at the time. This is what I wrote: 'I have written proof that Sid Fielden was planning my downfall before the Boycott suspension affair even blew up. I believe the whole thing was stage-managed at Scarborough, namely by pushing me into a corner where I couldn't back down as the television and media were on the ground within a few minutes and Sid Fielden just happened to have a petition ready for signing.' I also knew that Boycott, whether or not he was a tool in the hands of the Reform Group, was still sufficiently involved to have asked Brian Close during The Oval Test against Australia a week before the suspension business, whether he would be interested in taking over as Yorkshire manager if the Reform Group managed to get rid of me. It couldn't be coincidence, either, that Boycott and the Reformers held a cosy little meeting together during that Test.

But before I present my case, it will be worthwhile going back over the events as I saw them leading up to the suspension. We were in Scarborough, on and off, for about ten days at the start of September, being involved in the Fenner Trophy, which we eventually won by two runs in a thrilling final against Essex. Many weeks earlier I had told Boycott that, since he would probably be playing in the final Test, which was due to end on 1 September, he could, if he wished, take a rest for the Fenner, which started the day after the Test ended, and also miss a game we had arranged against a Barbados XI. I took quite a bit of time and trouble checking with Boycott during The Oval Test that this arrangement still stood – for, as usual, I found it almost impossible to get hold of him.

This may be hard to believe, but Yorkshire, his employers, and I, supposedly his boss, never had Geoffrey's home phone number, so I couldn't get hold of him before he left for The Oval. I did have the number once, but straightaway he changed it and I never had it again. As far as I know the only member of the Yorkshire staff who had his number at one stage was Arnie Sidebottom – I don't know what was so special about Arnie, but even he didn't keep it for very long.

I couldn't raise Geoffrey at the England team's hotel either and I never trust hotel message systems, so I asked Mike Gatting, who is a sensible sort of bloke, to pass on the word that our understanding stood – that Boycs would not be needed at Scarborough until the Northants game on 9 September. I don't know whether Mike, with his Cockney sense of humour, had taken the mickey a bit in front of the other England players, but it shouldn't have mattered if he had. What did happen was that Boycott was very upset, perhaps at having the message delivered by a third party. In any event, it ended with him telling all and sundry that I had dropped him from the Fenner Trophy, even though he knew weeks earlier that he wasn't going to play.

If ever I needed proof of that, it came when I rang the manager of the bookshop in York where Boycott uttered his infamous words about wanting a showdown. The manager confirmed that the appointment for Boycott to appear there and sign copies of his book had been made weeks in advance – so by doing it the day before the game against Northants was due to start was evidence that he knew he was not going to be needed in Scarborough until then.

The news of Geoffrey's outburst in the York bookshop reached my ears after we had played a charity match under the floodlights at the Scarborough football ground. It was a curtain-raiser for the Northants game which, if I remember rightly, was starting the next day.

We couldn't do anything about it that night, but next morning I gathered together all the facts I could before having breakfast with Chris Old, our skipper. I said to Chilly, 'I'm afraid I'll have to suspend him. What do you think?' He agreed completely.

I made a few phone calls – to Fred Trueman and Don Brennan, who were both on the Executive Committee, and they said, 'We agree entirely with you.' Michael Crawford, the chairman, was on holiday in Scotland. He subsequently told me that if he had been available he would have advised caution. But at the time he knew something I didn't know – and that's another story which I shall come to soon.

I went down to the Scarborough ground early and, though it was only 9 o'clock, Geoffrey Boycott was already there. I said, 'Regarding this stuff you said on TV last night, Geoffrey, I'm afraid you'll be suspended for this match and for the rest of the season. I'd like you to pack your bag and leave the ground now.'

In retrospect, I don't know whether Boycott really expected to be banned – for a man so dedicated to cricket, it seemed a high price to pay. But I know darned well the Reformers thought I would suspend him. In fact they must have been praying I would, because it was all part of their plan. Boycott didn't seem too bothered, though, hanging round the ground and signing autographs as the crowd started to come in. But for Jack Hampshire, this whole episode, together with the verbal attack on his wife, was the final straw as far as his relationship with Yorkshire was concerned, leading him to quit the county at the end of the season.

Boycott could have left long before anyone else came to the ground, but he was still there when Sid Fielden, attended by TV cameras which appeared from nowhere, began to organize a protest right there on the pitch which continued until the umpires went out to try and start the match. The atmosphere was so bad that when Shirley and our daughter Vicky arrived, two of the players, Bill Athey and Kevin Sharp, felt it necessary to go down to the car park to make sure they were safe.

So that was the end of the incident at the time. It wasn't until later, when the club committee held a special investigation into the whole business at the end of the season, that some of the mucky undercurrents began to surface.

It was at that committee meeting that I learned that Geoffrey Boycott should not have been playing at all for Yorkshire in 1981 since he had not signed the disciplinary clause in his contract – a fact that must have been known to the Reform Group and which, as further evidence bore out, they were planning to use to trap me. I believe that the York bookshop business was a ruse to entice me into suspending Boycott. The Reformers were then ready to turn on me and say I had no right to ban Boycott because he had not signed the clause in his contract which forbade him from making unauthorized statements to the media. What they failed to see in their anxiety to get rid of me was that Boycott had no right to be playing at all if he had not signed in its entirety the contract drawn up by the Test & County Cricket Board and issued to every one of England's 400 or so registered county cricketers.

June 1949. It seems a long time ago – but the little lad in the crumpled
gear *is* me and the score on the Farsley board *does* belong to me . . .
all made in a Priestly Cup game against Pudsey

Who's the good-looking young lad? Just turned twenty-six and all ready for a Test at Lord's in July 1958

All part of the job of skippering England – I introduce Geoff Boycott to the Queen during a Test at Lord's in 1971

Meeting the Queen again – only this time Shirley, Diane and Vicky came
with me when I received the CBE at Buckingham Palace in March 1973

Above: The old square cut looks like it was really working in this innings for Leicestershire in May, 1975. Then again, I don't reckon there's much wrong with the bowling action either . . . sideways on and left arm well up

Geoff Boycott as he would like to be remembered – he'd just made another hundred for England. This time it was against India at Edgbaston in 1979

Keith Fletcher did not deserve to lose the England captaincy. He could bat
too – as he shows New Zealand at Lord's

Below left: Keith Stackpole seems to have hit this one well enough – he
certainly hit the one from John Snow (below right) in Melbourne when he
was given 'not out' by umpire Max O'Connell

Time for a break with Graham Stevenson, Chris Old and David Bairstow
during a John Player League game against Middlesex at Lord's in 1980

We've won something at last! And the look on my face tells what it felt like to get my hands on the John Player League Trophy at Chelmsford in 1983

All pals together . . . Geoff Boycott and the rest of the Yorkshire lads in merry mood after winning

Jack Hampshire couldn't take the bickering and left for the quiet life in Derbyshire

Phil Carrick . . . I hope he hangs on to this one and on to the Yorkshire captaincy as well

The Reformers tried to say that I was so worried about the outcome that I had my own solicitor at that committee meeting. That's just not true – I have never had a lawyer at any cricket meeting I have been involved with as I have always found the men I have had to deal with honourable and trustworthy. There certainly were three lawyers present at this meeting – two of them, a solicitor *and* a barrister, were with Boycott. The third, John Bosomworth, was the club's own solicitor.

That meeting thrashed out some sort of statement which I felt let Geoffrey off lightly. So later the club officials, chairman Michael Crawford, captain Chris Old, myself, secretary Joe Lister and our solicitor met again to decide our next move. That was when Mr Crawford told us that if he had not been on holiday he would have advised caution – the reason being that he knew Boycott had not signed the disciplinary clause in his contract.

And that was the first time I had heard of it. I was furious, and so was Mr Bosomworth, the solicitor. He turned to Michael Crawford and Joe Lister (the only other person who knew) and said: 'Am I to understand that neither of you told the team manager that Boycott had not signed that part of his contract? If that is so, then I am disgusted.'

The Executive Committee, particularly Fred Trueman and Don Brennan, were darned angry, too, and they ruled that unless Boycott signed the entire contract as he was required to do, then he could not and would not play until he had. It seems amazing that such a situation could come about, but I'll explain what happened and why.

At the start of pre-season training I would take the contracts from Joe and give them to the players. They would look at them, sign them, and then hand them back for me to give them to Joe so that he could send them off to Lord's for registration purposes and so on. Boycott's, of course, had to go to his solicitor, Duncan Mutch, and it was always ages before you received it back. Eventually, I said to him, 'I haven't had your contract back yet, Boycs.' He said, 'I've given it direct to Joe.' I asked him, 'Are you sure?' and he said he was. So I said OK and that, as far as I was concerned, was the end of it.

It wasn't until this meeting at the end of the season that it all became clear. Geoffrey had crossed out all the disciplinary part and handed it direct to Joe so that I wouldn't see it. Joe must have told the chairman and between them they decided it was best to keep it in the dark for the sake of peace and quiet. They felt the whole business didn't matter too much, and if nobody made a fuss it would blow over in its own good time. Once again Yorkshire were being too nice and too weak – and once again by not being strong when they needed to be they dropped me and everyone else in the cart. By suspending Boycott we had done something which, strictly speaking, we had not been legally entitled to do. They knew that if they had told me about the contract I would have said: 'He signs it like everyone else or he doesn't play.' As it was, all they had done was lead me straight into the Reform Group's ambush.

And there was no doubt that an ambush had been set. As I said in my report to the committee: 'I have proof that they were planning my downfall before all this [the Scarborough suspension affair] even blew up.' In fact they were setting ambushes all the time – a group of them once even took a tape recorder and hid it under their table when I was giving a talk to the Saddleworth Cricket Club, just in case I let drop a comment that they might be able to use against me.

Peter Long, a Middlesbrough member I had never met before, though I think I'd seen him around at Yorkshire matches, was the man who tipped me off about the plot that was brewing at Scarborough. He has a good job with ICI and is the responsible sort of member I was beginning to think Yorkshire were fast running out of.

It was some time at the beginning of that momentous Scarborough fortnight that Mr Long sought me out during breakfast at the Royal Hotel. Even their excellent bacon and eggs had to take second place to what Mr Long had to tell me. It seems that only a few days earlier he had been sitting at Headingley, minding his own business, when a conversation started behind him that made him think that it was definitely his business not to mind his own business any longer. The conversation, between two men he did not know at the time, but who were, he was soon to discover, leading members of the Reform Group, and Mrs Gail Bairstow, former wife of David Bairstow, was quite clearly the first stage of an elaborate plot against me. Both Mr Long and I want to make it plain that the role of Mrs Bairstow – a garrulous lady who undoubtedly felt her husband was being hard done by in the Yorkshire captaincy stakes – was more of an informant than a plotter and was being used as such by the Reformers.

The full significance of what he had overheard did not come home to Mr Long until he attended a meeting called by the Reformers at Ossett on 6 September for no other reason than to make a fuss about my position as manager. The meeting was called, it is well worth noting, only two days before Geoffrey Boycott made his appearance in that book-shop in York and three days before the start of the match against Northants which he had to miss when I suspended him. Coincidence? Or a plot? I think that the letter which Mr Long wrote to Yorkshire chairman Michael Crawford the day after the Ossett meeting might throw some light on that:

> *Dear Mr Crawford,*
>
> *I was present yesterday at the open meeting of Yorkshire members called by the self-styled Reform Group. I entered with, like most members, misgivings about the present state of Yorkshire cricket, but I left plunged in pessimism for the future if this Group increases its influence.*
>
> *As may have been reported to you, a member from Hull and myself spoke in defence of Ray Illingworth. I do not know Illingworth personally but in another sense I seem to have known him for almost thirty years, from his earliest days with Yorkshire.*
>
> *I appeared at the meeting for only one reason. At the recent Roses match I overheard a conversation*

behind me which filled me with alarm for the well-being of the club. A man, whom I did not know, was conversing with a friend about the means of bringing about Ray Illingworth's downfall. To my dismay I became aware that the wife of one of the players was involved in this conversation – although only as a provider of background information.

I play and watch cricket, like all my family, for pleasure and I am not interested in club politics, but I resolved to do what I could to thwart this plot – indeed I turned round and said that anyone who wished to get rid of Illingworth should first be sure that they knew more about cricket than he did. Illingworth's appointment had seemed to me to be a decision to bring intelligence and purpose into Yorkshire cricket – his reputation among cricketers and cricket administrators is second to none.

I was unwilling to see this decision overthrown in favour of management by bar-room gossip and the mutterings of a player who, despite his admirable combative qualities, had shown himself to have more appetite than capability for the acting captaincy.

I therefore came to the meeting expecting that the 'plotter' would turn up. So he did, but you may imagine my surprise to see him sitting at the top table as secretary of the Reform Group! Subsequently I was not surprised when Mr Fielden, as I learned him to be, opened the meeting with a sustained diatribe against Ray Illingworth, later introducing snippets of dressing room tittle-tattle such as could only be obtained from a disaffected player. Contrary to Mr Fielden's view, I have seen Yorkshire very many times this year and they have appeared to be a happy team. I can well understand that this will not continue if Mr Fielden encourages players to vent and cultivate their grievances.

Many people at the meeting were, understand-
ably, much concerned by the lack of success of
the team under Illingworth's managership. Real
bigotry and hatred, however, appeared to be the
particular characteristic of those present who were
members of the Reform Group.

Sadly, events seem to be moving against Illing-
worth and I fear we shall lose him and, probably,
Hartley who in a couple of years' time could bring
intelligence and example to the Yorkshire captaincy
after serving an apprenticeship under the encourag-
ing hand of Chris Old.

I would, however, like you to regard this letter not
as essentially a plea for any individual, but rather
an appeal to the Yorkshire management, whatever
its failings, not to hand over the club to tap-room
bigots and the loudest-mouthed players. Not only
would this not bring the 'success' so much sought,
but the heart of Yorkshire cricket would be
destroyed.

A letter Mr Long wrote to the chairman three days later
further displayed the concern he felt over the plot that was
being hatched against me. In it he told Mr Crawford that he
had been so worried about what was going on that – and I
quote from his letter (with his permission) – 'I reported the
incident to the club secretary the following day. I attach a
copy of my letter to him. More recent events seem further
evidence that Mr Fielden revels in his own glorification even
if it means Yorkshire's ruination.'

On the same day, 10 September, Mr Long also wrote to the
secretary, Joe Lister:

Dear Mr Lister,
You will remember a brief discussion we had in
your office on Monday, 31 August, when I warned
you that I had overheard behind me during the
Roses John Player match a conversation obviously

plotting disruption within the club management and team.

Unfortunately a player's wife was involved – but, as I stressed, she seemed to be taking no part in the plot but was simply being used as a source of background information. At the time, as I explained, apart from the player's wife, I did not know the individuals involved.

I rather thought the chief 'plotter' would appear at the recent open meeting of the so-called Reform Group, and this proved to be the case. It turned out to be none other than Mr Fielden who at first denied all knowledge of the incident (I had angrily denounced this disruptive plotting, to the obvious consternation of the player's wife, but the two men, understandably, ignored my remarks). After the meeting Mr Fielden said to me that his friend had just reminded him of the incident (!).

This was my first contact with the Reform Group, but this seems to be an example of a thoroughly discreditable way of working. In view of the apparent official recognition of this unofficial group, I have written to the chairman of the management committee informing him of this incident. Yours sincerely, etc.

At the same time Mr Long wrote to me, enclosing a copy of the letter he had sent to Michael Crawford and saying: 'Although I have doubts about doing so, I enclose a copy of a letter which I have written to the chairman of the Yorkshire committee. On balance it seems only fair that you, the person most concerned, should have a statement about the Reform Group meeting other than just the usual press distortions. I would ask you to regard it as confidential and, of course, I hope that the unnamed player gets over his disappointment and works for the good of the team again.'

The gentleman from Hull whom Mr Long mentioned in his

letter to Michael Crawford was another of the silent majority who was gradually finding his voice. He did so in a letter to the *Yorkshire Post* the day after their report of the meeting at Ossett.

> *Sir,*
>
> *Because a handful of members, less than 1 per cent of the total membership, are dissatisfied with Yorkshire's results and meet to air their views, your newspaper gives the subject front-page prominence.*
>
> *Because I am disappointed with the county's lack of success I made a fifty-mile journey to attend the Ossett meeting. I am not a member of the Reform Group and indeed less than a dozen people at the meeting on a show of hands declared their membership of such a group.*
>
> *One person attempted several times to get a resolution approved demanding the resignation of the Yorkshire manager and he found scant support. The resolution carried expressed no confidence in the committee. Your newspaper was misleading when stating: 'The County's Reform Group passed a vote of no confidence in Ray Illingworth . . .'*

That letter was from Mr G. K. Denton, of Carr Lane, Willerby, Hull, to whom I am eternally grateful for pointing out the truth of what went on at the Post House Hotel in Ossett that Sunday in September, as well as giving me ample evidence of what I was saying earlier – that the *Yorkshire Post* was not always as strictly accurate and unbiased in its reporting as it claims to be and that it does indeed have a lot to answer for in the affairs of Yorkshire cricket. I am also eternally grateful to Mr Long for sending me a cutting of Mr Denton's letter. In so doing he supported Mr Denton's criticism of the report which said that a vote of no confidence in me had been passed. He agreed with Mr Denton's verdict that this was 'misleading' and said: 'Mr Fielden was supposed to convey this information to Lister on

Monday morning. It would be interesting to know if he reported accurately.'

It was also interesting to see that the Reform Group, foiled in their attempts to have Geoffrey Boycott crowned king there and then, were quietly backing David Bairstow for the captaincy – something which Bluey, especially after his row with me on the temporary appointment of Neil Hartley earlier that year, did nothing to prevent. The Reform Group did take up Bairstow's cause as early as June 1979, when Sid Fielden wrote a letter to Arthur Connell, who was chairman at that time, saying, amongst other things, 'Prior to the game at Northampton Illingworth is reported as saying that if Hampshire could not play and with Boycott and Old unavailable, he would consider taking over the captaincy himself. Does Illingworth consider that in such circumstances we have in Bairstow a player of international status who is quite capable of providing the inspirational leadership required and who ought to be given the opportunity to captain the side?'

Well, Bluey had to wait another two years after the Scarborough affair, two years in which I not only played, but also skippered Yorkshire and even won them a trophy, before he was given his chance, in 1984. It was a sad comment on Mr Fielden's knowledge of the game of cricket – or rather, lack of it – that he was unable to foresee the very problems that had made me so reluctant to give Bairstow, nice lad and keen though he is, the overall leadership. And Bluey, try though he might, could only keep it going for three years before November 1986 when, after finding his keeping was suffering, the committee relieved him of the captaincy.

Once again I was sorry, but not surprised, that the committee did not take the plunge and give the job to Hartley. But it went to Phil Carrick (Fergie) – and they could have done a lot worse. I'm sorry Carrick wasn't experienced enough to take charge when I was there – I could have worked with him.

The Yorkshire players knew Phil as 'Fergie' long before Prince Andrew made Sarah the Duchess of York, and I feel I had something to do with making this 'Fergie' into a class left-arm spinner. At least he thinks so. I don't think he'll mind me making public a letter he wrote to me when, in March 1984, I finally lost my job with Yorkshire. I received a stack of letters at that time, many of which I will be telling you about later, once we have wended our way through 1982 and 1983, and I reach those fatal days. But now, to end this chapter of letters, I'll let you into the one written to me in March 1984 by 'Fergie' Carrick – Yorkshire captain for the season 1987 – and I wish him the best of luck!

> *Dear Raymond,*
>
> *It was with great sadness and disappointment that I heard of your dismissal from Yorkshire CCC. May I take this opportunity in thanking you for giving back my confidence and self-pride in my bowling, which had been going nowhere for a year or two. The way in which you tackled cricket 'over 50' left me with nothing but admiration for you, especially in view of the constant barrage of abuse you had to endure.*
>
> *Had you not been in charge last year Yorkshire would not have won the John Player League, of that I am certain. For once in my career we played one-day cricket with spinners contributing significantly, whereas for years we did not play any at all in one-day cricket. Spinners, what are spinners? Thank you, Raymond Illingworth. It has been a privilege to have played with you and under your leadership. I will not forget! Regards, Fergie.*

Thank *you*, Fergie. I will not forget either . . . even as I now wade through the murky years of 1982 and 1983 that led up to the sacking you talk about in 1984.

8

CRITICISMS

I started off the 1982 season in a mood of guarded optimism. At the end of the previous season, following in the wake of the Scarborough scandal, the club's general committee made what was, at least, a token gesture towards sorting out some of Yorkshire's problems. Though I, as manager, was obviously going to be blamed for some of the things that had gone wrong, they did give me plenty of opportunity to put my side of the case. They gave me a one-year contract, as I had reached the end of my original three-year arrangement, and they formed a special sub-committee to carry out an in-depth investigation aimed at rooting out the reasons for why we were failing to win anything.

In all, that sub-committee had fifteen members and interviewed thirty-two people they thought might be able to throw some light on the darkness of Yorkshire cricket – and I was the first individual they spoke to. That was on 30 September 1981 – less than a fortnight after the formation of the sub-committee. Their other star witness was going to be Geoffrey Boycott – they were lining us up in opposite corners, so to speak. But the sub-committee found, as I so often did, that it was not so easy to find Geoffrey when you needed him. He had gone off on a trip to Hong Kong on Cathay Pacific, his own personal airline, before joining up with the England tour in India. Though he came home early from that tour when the manager, Raman Subba Row, found out for himself what life with Geoffrey could be like – especially

during the Calcutta Test which was the last one Boycott
ever played. But the sub-committee weren't to know that
and had already prepared an interim report without him.
They had tried to contact him in Bombay and had heard that
he had received their letter – though they didn't hear anything from him direct. So, knowing that Geoffrey would
eventually return and give his side of things, which he did on
20 January 1982, I reserved the right of reply, which I was
granted on 10 February.

The sub-committee were pretty upset by Boycott's non-
appearance before he went off to India. They recommended
that he was not given another contract until he *had*
appeared before the sub-committee and in their interim
report, prepared in his absence, said:

> *Immediately this committee was appointed, steps
> were taken by its secretary to arrange an appoint-
> ment with Mr Boycott prior to his leaving the UK for
> a holiday in Hong Kong before the India tour.*
>
> *In spite of telephone calls and a letter, we received
> no communication whatsoever from Mr Boycott,
> apart from one conversation on the telephone, and
> he must have appreciated the necessity of the com-
> mittee seeing him before he left the country to avoid
> any undue delay in the publication of this report to
> the full committee.*
>
> *Since then a communication was sent to Mr
> Boycott in Bombay asking him to answer a ques-
> tionnaire on a number of matters which this com-
> mittee had discussed. We are advised that he has
> received this letter, but no reply nor an ack-
> nowledgement has been received. We did receive
> communications from Mr Boycott's solicitor as we
> forwarded copies of our letters to Mr Boycott to
> him. It is for this reason and this reason alone
> that the committee thought fit to issue a first re-
> port, as obviously it would be unwise to complete
> our report without the opportunity of seeing Mr*

> *Boycott and obtaining his version of the many criticisms which we have received about him in relation to the Club.*
>
> *We have listened to much criticism of the present manager Mr Ray Illingworth, who was appointed to the post for the 1979 season on a three-year contract. It has been said that he had too many favourites, that discipline was applied to some and not to others and that the example he set by way of dress on some occasions left much to be desired, thus setting a bad example to some of the players.*

Well, I knew where the last part had come from, especially as the sub-committee had received two long-winded affidavits from Reform Group stars Sid Fielden and Peter Briggs who had spent most of the previous three years spying and writing down anything they felt they could use against me. Wherever I went a Reformer would pop up to check whether I had buttoned up my collar or fastened my fly properly. It was a wonder I didn't get as neurotic as they were, especially as there were times, on a hot summer day, when I did feel at liberty to slip my blazer off or loosen my tie after spending a couple of hours walking round the ground so as to get a good view of the cricket from behind the bowler's arm – at each end! Just to show you how niggling they became, they once moaned that I had gone out on the ground with a pint of beer in my hand at the end of play at Scarborough. True, I was on the ground with a beer in my hand, but it was only half a pint and I had rushed out to grab the groundsman before he went home to make sure he covered the bowlers' follow through properly.

That was where something else in the interim report pleased me. Despite the presence of one leading Reformer on the committee – Reg Kirk, who later became chairman of the club – they had come out with a strong criticism of the so-called rebels which, I felt, put me in a much better light with any outsiders who may not have been privy to exactly what was going on.

Ray Illingworth

This is what the report said – pure balm to my battered nerves:

> We believe that the presence of this body has done untold harm to the Yorkshire County Cricket Club. It has addressed itself to many matters of which it was not fully informed; it has made statements to the press and media which have been detrimental to the club.
>
> It has been suggested to us that the Reform Group was nothing more nor less than a 'Boycott fan club'. While we can understand a supporters club being formed with the object of raising funds, we believe that a group such as this, running in parallel to the club's committee and openly criticizing them to the extent they have done, is, to say the least, harmful to the club and its members. We are satisfied that the atmosphere which existed and in which the players' poll was taken would never have occurred but for the activities of the Reform Group and the divisive influence which its presence and its activities have fostered over a number of years. It may, however, be said that partly as a result of their representations this committee has been asked to carry out its present task. We recommend that the leading members of the Group, under whatever name, be advised that if they continue to carry on the Group's activities as they have done in the past, the Committee will consider invoking Rule 36 to expel them from the Club as members.

That was music to my ears and I spent hours picturing the arguments that must have gone on before Reg Kirk submitted to such a report. But, as usual, nothing was done about it, and the Reformers gained in power until, by 1984, they had control of the club and got rid of me.

The players' poll they talked about must have been the one carried out at the end of 1981 – at Hove, I think it was. That match against Sussex was our last Championship game of 1981 and came right after the scrap at Scarborough. The *Yorkshire Evening Post*, if I remember rightly, had put up the idea hoping, no doubt, that the outcome would be a resounding victory in favour of Boycott. Unhappily for them, an informal poll was held and the results of the three questions put to the players were: 'Would you like Geoff Boycott reappointed captain?' – fifteen were against and three abstained; 'Do you want to have Boycott in the side as a player next season?' – ten said no, two said yes, and four abstained; 'Do you want Raymond Illingworth to continue as manager?' – thirteen did and three abstained. You'd have thought that would have been enough for the club to throw their full weight behind me . . . but a couple of other things happened. One committee member, Eric Baines from Doncaster, resigned because he didn't think the result of the poll should have been made public. And guess who was elected in his place. None other than Sid Fielden!

But if some matters did seem to be running my way, it was inevitable that I should also come in for a fair amount of criticism. After all, Yorkshire weren't winning very much and I was their manager – charged with the responsibility of seeing that they did win something. The committee made a list of six reasons that they saw as being to blame for our failure to win anything. They each raise points that I feel I owe it to myself to answer.

These were the six criticisms that the 'in-depth' sub-committee made. To be fair, they were all genuine causes for concern – to me as well as to them. They also had the courage to accept that a proportion of the blame for Yorkshire's plight lay with the club itself, for their sixth and final point spoke of 'lack of leadership and decisiveness of the Committee'. If I had been preparing this report I think I would have put that one right at the top – as I have been stressing repeatedly, it was weakness, papering over the cracks, hoping things would sort themselves out, that had landed the county with the problems they were facing.

Let's take the points one by one, as they appeared in the

report. Their first point was this: 'A lack of true leadership of players both on and off the field since the departure of Mr Brian Close.' Well, all I can say is 'What did they expect?' I only ever had any real trouble with one player and he, after eight years in the captaincy, had created such a secure niche for himself that he was wellnigh fireproof. It got so bad by the end that if ever I told Geoff Boycott off I had to put it all down in writing – just so there couldn't be any arguments later about what had been said.

The second point was: 'Too many experienced players allowed to leave over a short time.' Right, dead right – except for one small detail. Jack Hampshire and Bill Athey, both England batsmen of the class we desperately needed, weren't *allowed* to leave – they both made up their minds they were going and that was that. There was nothing any of us could do to stop them. I tried, believe me, but when they gave their reasons there was little more I could say beyond 'Good luck!' There were times, many of them, when I wished I could have been going with them. But what upset me more was the way we were losing promising, often brilliant, youngsters, who couldn't see their careers ever likely to blossom in the stifling, heavy atmosphere that clouded the Yorkshire dressing room.

What also upset me was the committee's fourth point, which made out that I had shown a 'lack of thoroughness in spotting, recruiting and developing talented youngsters'. It was one of the unfortunate aspects of Yorkshire cricket that we did lose so many good players, and I am convinced that, but for the presence of Geoffrey Boycott, they would have either stayed with us having arrived, or else, as happened in several cases, would have joined us at the outset instead of pursuing their careers with other counties.

Wicket-keeper Steven Rhodes is one who should never have been allowed to go, though in his case it was more a case of becoming tired and dispirited at having to wait so long for his chance in the first team. I feel that it would have benefited everyone if David Bairstow had given up keeping to concentrate on his captaincy, and batting to keep young

Rhodes from going to Worcester, as he did at the end of 1984. Since then he has been, by all accounts, the outstanding personality, both on and off the field, of the England B tour to Sri Lanka in the winter of 1985–6 which should have earned him a trip to Australia in the winter of 1986 – why it didn't I'll never understand. Bairstow had already had his benefit, so he should have thought about Yorkshire's future. You can't afford to lose a player of Rhodes's ability – they come once every ten or fifteen years, if you're lucky!

I maintain that I did all any man could to find and nurture young talent for Yorkshire, and I still regret that two more managed to slip through the net. Tim Boon is a good player, born and brought up in Doncaster. We knew all about him, but he thought he'd be better off somewhere else (and who could blame him?) and in 1980 played his first game for Leicestershire. I'll tell you soon how I worked all hours God gave to find bowlers for Yorkshire, for that was where our main problems lay. So you can imagine my grief when Neil Mallender and his father Ron decided that he, too, would be better off at another county and he went to Northants.

Right from the day I joined Yorkshire as manager I set up a scouting system to try and find bowlers. We needed two more bowlers to come through and join the nucleus of good young players we already had – boys like Rhodes, Ashley Metcalfe, Paul Jarvis, Paul Booth and Martyn Moxon. With the help of a number of older senior players we could have had a good side again – but trying to rustle up a couple of bowlers out of nowhere was the sticking point. Berger Paints helped us with a 'Find a Fast Bowler' competition, held at seven or eight centres around the county. I called on a couple of players who knew all about bowling to help – Steve Oldham came back from Derbyshire and we always had Arnie Side-bottom, who helped out at the winter nets I set up at Leeds, Bradford and Barnsley. Anyone who wrote in for a trial was given one and we were receiving dozens of recommendations from league secretaries, club captains and so on. But to be honest, we were getting a load of rubbish – sent to us by people we thought had a bit of an idea about cricket.

The occasional youngster, like Phil Berry, an off-spinner who played for Young England, and Chris Shaw, did slip through. But Berry was only sixteen when I left so I don't know much about how he has progressed, and Shaw is no more than a fourth seamer at best. Yet we spent four nights a week at those winter nets – and the 'in-depth' sub-committee said we didn't try! There simply wasn't that much talent around – that's all there is to it.

The third point the committee made brings me to a subject that really gets up my nose – overseas players. They were kind enough to blame Yorkshire's poor results partly on 'the increase of international players in other counties'. Well, Yorkshire, of course, not only refuses to have players from other countries, they won't even take them from other counties! This, of course, makes it harder to find a winning team, even though Yorkshire is bigger than most counties and has a great cricket tradition. It would have been a lot easier if I had been able to go out and sign a West Indian fast bowler, but it was up to the members to decide whether they wanted to go outside the county and when it was put to the vote the idea was roundly defeated. There was talk a couple of years back about Malcolm Marshall joining us when his contract with Hampshire ran out but that was all it was – talk. I'm not saying I would have been against the idea if it had been possible. It would have certainly made my job easier and there were people, both inside and outside the club, who were all for the idea. But with the rules as they stood it was impossible.

I'm not going into all the pros and cons of having overseas players in county cricket. Those arguments have been pretty well thrashed out many times. But I do know that if I was in charge of cricket in this country I would see that players from countries that don't want us would not be allowed to make their livings here. Look at that England B tour of Sri Lanka we talked about. They were meant to go to Zimbabwe and Bangladesh as well, but they were told not to go almost as they set off for the airport. Yet those countries had been made welcome here for the World Cup the summer before.

Look at Guyana. They stopped England playing there because we had Robin Jackman in our team in 1981. We didn't
even try to go there in 1986 – and their Sports Minister, who
served the deportation order on Jackers, was none other
than Roy Fredericks, who had made his living playing
county cricket for Glamorgan some years ago. Some of the
fellows who were there in 1981 tell me he was so ashamed he
didn't know where to put his face. I know that if I was that
ashamed at the job I was doing I would jack it in pretty
darned quick.

The fifth point was: 'The lack of team spirit and "Yorkshire
dedication" partly fostered by the existence of the Reform
Group.' Well, anyone who takes the time and trouble to read
this book will know what I feel about that. I hope they will
agree, too. And the sixth point was: 'The lack of leadership
and decisiveness of the Committee.' Well, what could you
expect when we had committees with so many members, all
trying to keep their respective areas of this great big county
happy, that it looked more like Leeds v. Hull Kingston
Rovers when they all scrummed down together? That was
why we had to form the special three-man 'trouble shooting'
committee of Ronnie Burnet, Fred Trueman and Billy Sutcliffe to handle day-to-day problems as they arose. Without
them we would never have got a decision on anything.

So far so good. But on the field of play, which is really what
everything else is all about, things weren't going so well and
getting worse – with the result that Chris Old had to be
sacked from the captaincy and I took over for the match
against Essex at Ilford on 23 June 1982. The truth is, I'm
afraid, that Chilly hadn't been looking after himself in the
way that any professional sportsman, particularly a fast
bowler, should. Day after day he would arrive at the ground
and slump in his seat in the dressing room, looking like
death warmed up. People like Bill Athey would say, 'Come
on, Chilly, buck up!' But he would just groan and say, 'I don't
feel too well today.' By teatime he was as often as not bright
and perky again – but by then it was always too late.

We didn't just give him the 'chop' – far from it. We gave him every chance to pull himself together. Ronnie Burnet and I had him in the office at Leeds and said we weren't very happy with the way things were going. We told him he had two weeks in which to show some improvement, but in that fortnight matters went from bad to worse. By then our results had put us out of contention for both the Championship and the John Player League, but it needed a horrendous weekend against Northants at Middlesbrough to bring matters to a head. It was a hell of a weekend – a right débâcle. We looked a real shambles. Geoff Cook and Wayne Larkins started the three-day match with an opening stand of 278, the highest ever for Northants against us. It wasn't the size of the stand that angered me – it was the way the runs came. They didn't have to bat. They just slogged us around – the bowling was all over the place and I felt thoroughly ashamed.

The game on Sunday was every bit as bad. Cook and Larkins put on 128 this time as Northants made 282, the highest total ever against Yorkshire in that competition. Allan Lamb smashed 5 sixes and 6 fours as he raced to 67 off only 36 balls. It was terrible – and something had to be done. And the next week, as soon as the county game was over, we did it. Chilly was relieved of the captaincy and the committee asked me to take over at Ilford – fifteen days after my fiftieth birthday.

I would still have been happy at that time for Neil Hartley to take over, but there was so much political in-fighting going on I couldn't bring myself to ask him. It wouldn't have been fair. Ronnie and Fred were at some kind of 'do' the previous weekend and six or seven of the committee who were also there came to the conclusion that the only answer was for me to come back and play for a while to sort out the mess – at least to organize things and get them back on an even keel.

We did manage to get things a bit more organized – field placings set, people knowing where to stand and what was expected of them and looking more like cricketers again. It was the middle of the season by then and, as I have said, too late for us to win anything.

But we were beginning to look like a team again, and even if we lost a match at least we didn't lose stupidly. We were able to control sides again – we were no longer being smashed out of sight. The first two games, against Essex and Notts, were ruined by the weather, and Derbyshire did make 473 against us at Derby – with John Wright hitting a career best 190. But they never got away from us and the match was not lost – and we won enough to pull ourselves up to tenth in the table.

We were lucky that Arnie Sidebottom had his best season for fitness – bowling almost 500 overs in the Championship and taking 62 wickets – but that was balanced by injuries to Alan Ramage, Graham Stevenson and Chris Old, who spent much of the summer coming in off his Sunday run.

Yet we still reached the semifinals of the NatWest Trophy and we were a bit unlucky having to bat first on a rain-affected wicket against Warwickshire which led ultimately to a 7-wicket defeat – our second in a semifinal since I had gone back to Yorkshire. It had rained all night at Edgbaston and we did well to make 216 after being 52–4, 81–5 and 99–6. Geoff Boycott came into his own in situations like that and this time he batted right through the collapse for 51. It was a lot easier when Warwickshire batted and they knocked them off in 55.3 overs with Andy Lloyd making 66 and David Smith 113.

I don't think the players were either surprised or sorry that the change was made and I became captain. It hadn't been easy for them – especially the younger ones like Bill Athey and Kevin Sharp. They like to have someone to look up to and they needed a man at the helm who wasn't going to be outgunned and outmanoeuvred. There is nothing worse in life than a cricket match that is sliding rapidly away from you like a roller-coaster and there's nobody in your team who can do a thing to stop it.

I think most of them expected it – Bill Athey saw me bowling for an hour or more in the nets at Middlesbrough and he said: 'I know what you're up to. You're going to play again, aren't you?' They were happy – they'd been worrying the life out of me for ages to come back and give it a go. But it wasn't easy. I had joined in the pre-season training and after that I'd bowled a bit in the nets and done my share of jogging with the lads. But this was the end of June and I'd gone a couple of months without doing anything too strenuous. Still, my confidence was given a boost when in my first match I took the wickets of two Test players – John Wright and Jack Hampshire – taking 2–36 against Derbyshire at Derby on 27 June 1982.

9

THE CHELTENHAM AFFAIR

The next season, 1983, was the last in many ways: my last as manager and captain of Yorkshire, my last as a professional county cricketer – and the last year of my life that was unhappy. Things were changing at Yorkshire. Chris Old, released at the end of the previous season, had joined Warwickshire and gave them one year's good service, which is what I had told David Brown, their manager, to expect from him – just as a way of showing he could still turn it on when he wanted. And we won something – for the first time in fourteen years – when the John Player League trophy found its way to Headingley. It was a triumph welcomed by most level-headed people in the county, but totally ignored by the Reform Group who were much more interested in the fact that we finished bottom of the County Championship.

I'm sure their members will be reading this for the failures, so that's where I'll start. The Benson & Hedges was the Reform Group's first triumph, but though we failed to qualify, we didn't really do all that badly. The game against Notts at Leeds was tight – they made 195–8 in their 55 overs and we were all out for 170 with 4 overs left. The game against Lancashire looked pretty bad on paper, with them making 222–6 and our reply being 87–5 off 35.4 overs. The truth was that it was a rain-affected match and we spent our entire innings watching the clouds and trying to judge when it would rain and how many runs we would need when it did. In the end, as so often happens, we fell between two stools. In fact, there was no play at all on the second day. If there had been we might possibly have won.

I didn't play in the third qualifier against Warwickshire at Edgbaston. Again it was very wet and we played four seamers plus Phil Carrick. Looking back in the records I see that they did the same – four quicker bowlers, plus Norman Gifford. The game itself was reduced to 45 overs each. We made 224–5 and they knocked them off for 5 wickets in 42.1 overs – not a bad result and further proof of the captaincy ability of Neil Hartley, who stood in for me that day.

In the Championship we won only one match – but we lost only five, which was the same as Essex, who won the title. And there were a lot of games that, with another half an hour, we might well have won, and two or three wins can send you shooting up the table. Of the five we lost, two were declaration games so there is nothing to be ashamed of there.

But the real excitement of 1983 came, as was so often the case, in the last month or so of the season with the now notorious Cheltenham affair, which was in effect the catalyst which finally brought about my departure from Yorkshire, and a wet and windy day at Chelmsford when, without a ball being bowled and hardly anyone even finding it necessary to change into whites, we won the John Player League.

A lot has been written and spoken about Saturday, 13 August, the first day of our match against Gloucestershire at Cheltenham which goes to show that everyone, even if they were not in full possession of the facts, at least knew and understood the importance of that day to me and to Yorkshire cricket. It was, in a nutshell, the day that broke the camel's back – that particular camel being me.

I knew it was going to be one of those days, with Geoffrey Boycott in one of those moods, before the match even started. We had arranged for a team photograph to be taken – blazers and all – some time before the start of the first day. Geoffrey, no doubt, would have been happier looking at the pitch, testing the breeze and psyching himself up for his innings –

but there was no need for him to swear and be so rude as he was, first to one small boy, and then to a group of others, who politely asked for his autograph. I had to tell him he was out of order and, worse still, a number of Gloucestershire members had heard him swear and I was called upon to apologize to them as well.

It wasn't the ideal way to start a game in such a pleasant and genteel spot as Cheltenham. But at least Geoffrey found a way to avoid any more hassle – he spent the entire day at the wicket, making 140 not out in our total of 344–5 declared, spending 375 minutes and facing 347 balls to do so on a good pitch, a small boundary and fast outfield. It was about mid-afternoon that we became really bogged down, but at least we had Kevin Sharp (Sharpie) going well. He hadn't made a century for three years, and he had gone in the best part of two hours after Boycott, yet he still got to his 100 first.

There were about 7 overs left when we finally got our third batting point, but I wanted all 4, since we were near the bottom of the table and every point was vital. In fact, the way it eventually turned out, our failure to make that fourth batting point was what finally sent us to the bottom of the table where, of course, we stayed – for the first time in Yorkshire's history. So I started to make signals which were basically aimed as suggestions to Geoff that he pulled his finger out and got a so-and-so move on. Geoff, unfortunately, didn't see it that way – in fact he chose not to see my signals at all. So I concentrated on Sharpie and he, of course, got the message which, since he promptly marched down the pitch and engaged Geoffrey in earnest conversation, he soon conveyed to Boycott.

Boycott's response, whether in a spirit of revenge or born of a genuine desire to secure that extra point, was to push one firmly, but not too firmly, in the direction of mid-wicket, who was saving the single, and calling Sharpie for a run. He was stuffed by the length of the M1. Graham Stevenson, promoted for a quick dart, came and went – and so did our fourth batting point. But there were still thirty-five minutes left –

time to push on for a big enough score to give us a chance to declare and perhaps even win the match.

By then Jim Love was in with Boycott and I sent out word with twelfth man Nick Taylor for them to make as many as they could before the close. By then we had only lost about 4 wickets and there was no excuse for hanging around. What happened then is the reason that Boycott was reprimanded at a later date, that the Reform Group were roused to fury that their man should be so shabbily treated, and that I, less than a fortnight later, threatened to quit Yorkshire.

Taylor tried to talk to Boycott, who told him: 'Go and talk to the other man, he's the senior player.' What he meant by that I cannot imagine, except that when the committee came to discuss the whole business in Leeds a week later, on Friday, 16 August, they telephoned Love and asked him to appear. When he got there Love confirmed that Taylor had passed on the message and that Boycott had said: 'I'll continue batting in my own way.' And that's what he did, making 6 runs in the last half hour when he had already been in all day and was under instructions to get a move on.

Boycott has since said that I should have taken the orders out to him personally. I ask you! When did you last see a captain or manager go out to the middle himself to deliver instructions to a batsman? Boycott's supporters say he should never have been reprimanded by the peace-keeping committee of Ronnie Burnet, Fred Trueman and Billy Sutcliffe. What should we have done . . . given him a bonus for flagrantly flouting orders?

I can tell them now that the committee almost didn't do anything. I know chairman Ronnie Burnet was getting cold feet about landing the club in more trouble by reprimanding Boycott and it was only when Jim Love told the committee just how defiant Geoffrey had been that he was pushed into action. The Reformers were angry that Boycott was not told personally. But it was the same old story – where on earth was he when you needed him?

Imagine the scene. We were upstairs at Headingley and the press were waiting downstairs in the bar, becoming more

and more impatient as the pints went down and the dead-
lines grew nearer. We had to tell them something – and it
had to be the truth. Boycott had been reprimanded, like it or
not.

The Reform Group in their anxiety to find whipping boys,
also turned on the press, at least those who had not thrown in
their lot with the Boycott cause. And the story which has
reached me of the experiences of David Warner, cricket
writer of the *Bradford Telegraph and Argus*, a nice fellow
who writes things as he sees them, bears this out. Warner
was spotted at Cheltenham on the day in question – by Sid
Fielden, of course – having a word with me as he walked back
from the pavilion with a cup of tea for one of the boys in the
press box who had an injured leg and was unable to fetch it
for himself. 'Are you going to report Geoffrey?' Warner
asked. 'I can't say,' I replied. 'You had better draw your own
conclusions.' And he did, writing in his paper that, in his
opinion, there was a chance Boycott would be reported to the
committee for slow scoring.

Now it was Warner's turn to come under the Reformers'
spotlight. They knew he had spoken to me – and they were
desperate to find out what it had all been about. That night
David knew I was having a meal at a steak house near the
team's hotel and set off to walk there in order to see if I had
anything further to say about Boycott's innings. Unknown
to Warner, Sid Fielden, using all his detective's cunning,
followed him, dodging in and out of cover so as not to be
discovered, even hiding at one stage so that David, who had
started behind him, could get in front. David tells me he had
asked Peter Briggs, another senior Reformer, to accompany
him to the steak house as a witness to anything that might be
said, but Briggs excused himself on the grounds that his
dinner was on the table getting cold. When David reached
the restaurant he peered through the window and saw that I
was eating with some of the players and, polite as he is,
decided not to go in and returned to the hotel where he was
'arrested' by Fielden, who wanted to know everything he had
been up to.

They had to wait until the Friday before they knew it all. That was when the peace-keeping committee announced:

> *We have had a long discussion with Boycott and listened to his version of events and at his request obtained evidence from other people. We are satisfied that in this instance his batting was not in the best interests of the side and again he has been told that at all times he must play the sort of innings the side needs irrespective of his own ambitions.*

That did it. The Reform Group went mad. Boycott went out and in the next match, against Notts at Park Avenue, hit 163 and 141 not out to become the first player in Yorkshire's history to make 100 in each innings twice against the same opponents. When, during another match against Gloucestershire at Scarborough the following week, the Reformers started talking about yet another petition, this time to re-open the Cheltenham affair, I announced I would quit.

Sid Fielden was writing to Joe Lister, he was writing to chairman Michael Crawford, he wanted another special meeting of the general committee – and I was fed up with it. I couldn't make a decision, whether as captain or manager, without having to explain myself to any Tom, Dick or Harry who elected himself as my judge – especially if it concerned one GB. So on 26 August, the final day of that Scarborough game against Gloucestershire, I let it be known that I was going to go.

I didn't tell the committee at that stage, but I meant it just the same. I simply released a statement in which I said, if I can remember the exact words: 'I don't see why I should be playing first-class cricket at the age of fifty-one to try and help Yorkshire and at the same time have to put up with a constant barrage of attacks from Boycott supporters on how I am handling the game.' I'm sure the Reformers felt Christmas had come four months early, but the flood of letters I received from true Yorkshire supporters made me wonder if I was doing the right thing. And that, if I am honest, is probably the reason I hedged my bets some three weeks later at Chelmsford when we won the John Player League. Perhaps it was the excitement of Yorkshire's first trophy for fourteen years, perhaps it was the champagne, but I said I would continue as Skipper on some kind of part-time basis if they wanted me. But as things turned out, they didn't want me. I was happy about that, but I was sorry for the fine folk who had written to me that August when they thought I was going, and also the following spring when they knew that I had.

I make no apologies for including a number of letters I received just after the Cheltenham affair and, most of them, within hours of my threat to resign. Without exception they come from ordinary Yorkshire folk, anxious only to see their county play well, play hard but, above all, play fair . . . Typical were letters from two men – one directed to me, the other to the *Yorkshire Post*.

Mr John Light, a headmaster at a school in Plymouth, wrote to me, saying:

> *I write as one who saw G. Boycott's innings at Cheltenham. Surely the aim of a county side batting on the first day is to: (a) get in a winning position; (b) earn as many bonus points as possible. It was obvious that G. Boycott was interested in doing neither, just playing to be not out. What you, as captain, can do when your leading batsman takes that attitude, I do not know. It amazes me that the man has so many supporters and followers. I sympathize with you utterly. Best of luck for the future.*

Mr F. N. Ibbotson, of Harrogate, wrote his letter to the *Yorkshire Post*, and complained, as I did earlier, of the weight of letters in that paper which supported the Reform Group while those which were opposed to their views were conspicuous by their almost complete absence. Says Mr Ibbotson:

I have read so many letters in your paper supporting the Mr G. Boycott case in the dispute with Mr R. Illingworth without a single letter in support of Ray Illingworth that I felt the following was somewhat overdue.

One cannot dispute the statistical record of Geoff – he is a run machine, but in this present-day cricket, particularly the 'overs' limitation, there is so much more to the game than accumulating runs over a prolonged period. I think that last Sunday's Players League match against Derbyshire serves to illustrate my point – Yorkshire were asked to score 169 to win the game in 40 overs, a reasonably modest target of fractionally over 4 runs per over when Boycott went to the crease. When he left, after 10 overs, he had scored 8 runs out of a total of 15, so that the asking rate was 154 runs in 30 overs. It just isn't good enough to say he had to see the shine off or that he usually anchors the innings – the fact is that Geoff spends far too long in settling to the detriment of the team. They simply cannot afford the luxury of even one over to get a sight of the ball and at times are often expected to 'blast off' as soon as they get to the crease after G.B. has consumed too many overs – just ask the lads!

So that when one compares G.B.'s average with the other recognized batsmen, one is just not comparing like with like (G.B. goes serenely on, intent on his own record regardless of bonus points or the resultant asking run rate. The other lads are expected to commit suicide, or almost, as soon as they arrive at the wicket).

If it is argued that G.B., as an opening bat, should do just that, then I would say that Gooch, Greenidge, Barlow, Slack, Stovold and Hassan are also opening bats – compare their runs per over with G.B.'s. Frankly I feel that the whole situation can be summarized thus: the innings of Bill Athey and

The Cheltenham Affair

Kevin Sharpe last Sunday against Derbyshire and David Bairstow and Arnie Sidebottom today against Middlesex were far more meritorious than many of G.B.'s selfish centuries. I would even go further and suggest that if Geoff was given the option of scoring a century in a match which his team loses or a duck when his team wins, he would opt for the former.

I don't think it would be right for me to comment any further, except to say that I've looked up the two matches Mr Ibbotson was talking about. The Derbyshire game was in the John Player League. It was at Bradford and we won by two wickets after being in trouble, thanks to a brave 21 not out from Bill Athey, who batted with a runner after being injured in a car accident the night before, and a quickfire 56 from Kevin Sharp.

The Middlesex match was at Leeds and was a Championship game. Boycott started it needing 60 runs to make 1,000 in the month of August. Suffice it to say that when he was out for 44 we were well below two runs an over on a docile pitch, and it needed a stand of 133 in 33 overs between Bluey and Arnie, who made 78 going in at number five to give us a total of 293 and only two batting points.

It would be easy to say that the lack of letters supporting me in the *Yorkshire Post* was because there weren't any . . . not so. As I have said before, many people told me they had written to the paper to back me up, but their letters never appeared. If I needed proof of that, it was provided in the couple of days following my threat to resign. Here are just a few of the letters I received that last week of August 1983. Ever the gallant one, that's me, the first I will mention was from a lady, Mrs Joyce Kent, of Bridlington. This is what she wrote:

May I, as a lifelong cricket lover, say how very sorry I am about the latest turn of events. Boycott is like a young cuckoo, pushing out one after another of the rightful occupants of the nest. I'd like to put him and his supporters into a one-way rocket to Mars!

I do sincerely hope that you will stay and have a happier time until you finally retire. If you are driven to going, may I say a very big 'thank you' for all you have done for Yorkshire, for cricket, and for all the people who have enjoyed watching you play.

Mr C. G. Leyland, from Leeds, wrote me a long letter. But the part which perked me up most was when he made it clear that he, and many other Yorkshire supporters, were aware of the problems that not only I, but my family, were going through. This is what he said:

Despite all the aggro you and your family suffer, can I make a plea with you not to resign. I can quite see that the Brother Scargill (Fielden) of the Yorkshire committee will soon have another bright idea, and that will be to put Boycott in your position should you go, and that would be the end of Yorkshire CCC.

This Fielden, along with Briggs, and that chap from Bradford (plus such as Callaghan of the Evening Post*) does not seem to understand cricket at all. Here we are with the finest batsman in the world (or so they tell me) and there is only one team with less bonus points for batting, and I get into arguments galore about Boycott and, until I point out how slow he goes, they never look at it my way. They first look at the paper, see how he has done, and then what the rest have done – and then all you get is: 'If it wasn't for Boycott . . .'*

I tell them they should have sacked him four years ago, and though you may not agree with this, I still think there is enough talent there, and the team spirit would be better, and I would rather have fourteen or fifteen available of equal standing, working with pride *for Yorkshire and not for self glory.*

The Cheltenham Affair

Surely some of the team must get fed up hearing about Boycott. I do believe that this year he has been responsible for us not winning more matches – like Leicester (twice), Derbyshire, Gloucestershire, Notts and at least one Sunday match which will prove vital at the end of the season.

I'm happy to say that Mr Leyland was overpessimistic about our chances in the Sunday League because, as we know now, we did win it that season. But the point about sacking Geoffrey is interesting. I do know that it was only the casting vote of the then chairman, John Temple, that kept him with the county as long ago as the mid-1970s. I also know, because I have seen a letter written by one county in response to his approach, that in the late 70s and early 80s, after I had gone back to Yorkshire and he had lost the captaincy, he was always trying to find a county that would have him. I even remember a story in the *Sun* about that time saying there was a chance of Geoffrey joining Lancashire. It was strongly denied from all directions – but I am sure there was more than an element of truth in it.

But back to Mr Leyland, who tells me he once had a chat with me at Headingley, interrupted only by the catcalls of the Reformers. I remember that, Mr Leyland, so please go on:

What worries me is that some committee men might follow you, and that would let in more Reformers. I think that Fielden has a right cheek calling for the resignation of Ronnie Burnet, a man who has done a lot for Yorkshire, though I sometimes wish he was as strict now as he was when he captained the county.

And what is going to happen about Neil Hartley now? He doesn't seem to be able to hit form at all and there are people who would have Boycott back again as captain, but I thought Hartley handled the team very well when you missed the Notts match. Well,

*here's hoping you will stay with the county and
people will begin to see sense again.*

Well, Mr Leyland, Ronnie Burnet did leave the committee,
but only after being beaten in the elections of the following
winter, something I will deal with later. But what I will say
now is that the day Yorkshire members voted out Ronnie
Burnet, they lost themselves one of the finest men they have
ever had.

Mr Robert Gibbs, from Knaresbrough, seems to agree with
me. This is what he wrote to me:

> *I just want to say that in common with hundreds of
> others I agree with your disciplining of Boycott for
> his repeated slowness in batting. It seems to me a
> better method of disciplining him would be to drop
> him for a match following a 'go-slow' because this
> would hit him where it hurts most. It would de-
> crease his chances of getting 1,000 runs in a month
> or his 2,000 in a season and at the same time lessen
> his chances of improving his average by getting a
> big 'not out' score. At the same time I feel sure it
> would improve the* team's *batting performance by
> getting rid of what must be a deadweight with a
> deadening effect. I also agree with Mr Burnet when
> he says that there is no hope for Yorkshire cricket so
> long as Boycott's crank supporters are around. You
> and your family have my deepest sympathy.*

It was good to know that people were aware of just what my
family had been through and it was largely with them in
mind that I made my threat to resign. As Mr D. S. Duffy, of
Ossett, wrote:

> *I sincerely hope that your family are not subjected to
> the same treatment by the idiots that they were two
> years ago. I have the highest regard for them and
> they had my sympathy during the often personal*

bitter attacks on you. The people responsible for those comments are not real Yorkshire supporters.

Mr Eddie Lawler, of Leeds, admitted to me:

I honestly thought your 'comeback' would be folly. It wasn't. So I write to say, 'please don't become despondent.' I think you have a lot to give to the game, and thereby, to people. It is more than unfortunate when people like Jack Hampshire and possibly yourself, are alienated by head-hunters and chauvinists who can't put two and two together. The YCCC set-up needs radical change and the appointment of a manager was at least a step in the right direction.

And finally Mr Robert Way, who said he was seventy-one the day he wrote the letter and was exiled to Baslow in Derbyshire:

I am just writing you a letter assuring you of my support and, I am sure, that of many other county members in your first-class captaincy of Yorkshire as well as in your tenure of the manager's appointment. I think you are doing a great job in circumstances which you must find exasperating at times and I do urge you to take no notice whatsoever of the loud-mouthed and ignorant gentlemen, whether on the committee or not, who seek to court publicity for themselves by suggesting that you are not.

Less than two weeks after all those letters were written we won the John Player League. It was the warmheartedness of those members that caused me to make my offer to stay on in some capacity – if Yorkshire wanted me. Only the events of the following winter saw to it that they didn't.

10

RUN OUT

It was not long before the thunder from Cheltenham began to echo around Headingley and suddenly all the drama that had been building up during the past five years exploded with one almighty bang. The events of the winter of 1983–4 have been well chronicled – Boycott's sacking, David Bairstow being made captain, the vote of no confidence in the committee, the elections at which the Reform Group, by virtue of a well-oiled publicity machine, took over the club, Boycott's reinstatement and finally – and inevitably – my dismissal.

What hasn't been so well recorded was my part in all these momentous events. The first moment of high drama was the meeting on 3 October of the cricket committee which voted unanimously to release Geoff Boycott, to make Bairstow captain and to ask me to revert to my original duties as team manager. The same afternoon the general committee confirmed the cricket committee's decisions by a two to one majority.

As manager I was, of course, closely consulted on these decisions and though I was not in entire agreement with all of them, I made no objections since they certainly represented a giant step forward. My contribution was to withdraw my threat to resign made the previous August. I had to agree that I would no longer play for Yorkshire though I still felt that, as I said after we won the John Player League, I might have something to offer in one-day cricket. I even felt I could still be useful in six or seven Championship matches per season – especially the ones where the pitch and the conditions cried out for two spinners, one of whom could have been me.

But I knew what they were up to – and since it was so important for the club I wasn't going to make life difficult for them. Three or four of the committee had made up their minds ever since Cheltenham that Boycott had to go and at last they drew the rest behind them. They were only making Bluey captain to divert some of the flak they knew would follow their decision. I still think Neil Hartley was the boy, but to be rid of Boycott was so important I was prepared to go along with them on Bairstow. They knew my feelings. They were that as long as Boycott played for Yorkshire there was no way forward for the club; he split players, the committee and supporters right down the middle. It could not continue, though the Reform Group thought it could.

Four hundred Yorkshire members, almost all of them Reformers, piled into the Post House at Ossett – I wish I'd bought shares in Trust House Forte! They demanded that the committee thought again and changed its mind – and to hell with the fact that it was costing the club a fortune and that the committee was a properly elected democratic body anyway!

That was on 9 October. On 16 October the cricket commit-tee, obedient to the wishes of the Ossett 400, met again – and again they ratified, this time by 18 votes to 8, the same things they had decided on a fortnight earlier. Just to make sure the fact would sink into even the most hardened 'rebel' head, chairman Michael Crawford issued a statement which I will give in full since it reflects my own views at the time very neatly:

> *In reaching their respective decisions the commit-*
> *tees had to take into account the fact that over the*
> *past few years the club has not succeeded in achiev-*
> *ing results satisfactory to Yorkshire members until*
> *the winning of the John Player Special League this*

year. It has always been recognized that there come times when older players must give way to younger players so that the club can give its more promising youngsters the chance to show what they can do without the risk of losing them to Yorkshire cricket. The committees are most anxious to ensure that the young players now coming into the side should not be subjected to a background of dissension and discord which creates a lack of confidence and a form-destroying atmosphere and to ensure also that the achievements of all members of the team are given equal and fair recognition.

I should point out at this stage that Bill Athey had just announced that he could not see matters improving at Yorkshire and had decided to pursue his career elsewhere. The statement goes on:

During the course of the year soundings were taken as to the possibility of Geoff Boycott retiring at the end of next season for which he had already been granted a testimonial. Geoffrey indicated (and he confirmed this at a meeting with Mr Crawford and Mr Burnet on Friday last, 14 October) that it was at that time his wish to continue playing after next season, and it had been his hope that he would regain his place as an opening batsman for England.

The general committee had taken its decision to award Geoffrey Boycott a testimonial independently of any decision in regard to his contract because it was felt that the members of the club and the cricket-loving public should have the opportunity of showing their appreciation of Geoff Boycott's years of service to the county since his benefit in 1979.

Regrettably, after the Cheltenham affair, the position deteriorated. A matter which in other counties would have been considered of minor importance became a burning issue. Bickerings started again, rancour became public and inevitably the atmosphere in the dressing room once more suffered. Bearing in mind the difficulties faced in retaining younger players and the urgent need to restore team harmony and morale, the committees decided that a start must be made to rebuild a younger Yorkshire team in order to re-establish Yorkshire's position as one of the premier cricket-playing counties.

The county was fortunate in having two established opening batsmen in Geoffrey Boycott and Richard Lumb. It had another of high potential in Martyn Moxon and another of very promising talent in Ashley Metcalfe. Young players such as these cannot be kept in the background and retained. With this in view, Ray Illingworth was not re-appointed captain and will devote himself to his duties as manager to which he was originally appointed. David Bairstow was made captain and Geoffrey Boycott was not offered another contract. These decisions were each dependent one upon the other. Moreover the committee have had to take into account the real possibility of established players following Bill Athey's decision not to stay with the club.

Whilst fully aware before they took their decisions of the strong feelings which would be aroused in regard to Geoffrey Boycott and of which they have been made aware since they made their decision, the two committees are convinced that the necessity to build team spirit for the good of Yorkshire cricket must override the interests of any one individual, however able and proficient that person may be. The committee believe that those who know their cricket and have the best interests of Yorkshire cricket at heart will agree that, unfortunate though that may be for a player such as Geoff Boycott, the right decision has been taken. The committee are appre-

ciative of support given by persons who are not only public figures but are, most important of all, knowledgeable cricketers or cricket watchers. The committee are aware that 2.5 per cent of members are able to requisition a special general meeting. If such a requisition is received the committee are fully prepared to justify their decision to members of the club. The cost to the club will be enormous, not only in terms of money. The damage to the morale of players is greatly underestimated by those who support Geoffrey Boycott, people who do not have all the background information and who are not as well informed as those who had to take the decisions.

It must not be forgotten that the members have elected the General Committee. The members have given to the General Committee the power to manage the club. The General Committee intend to manage the affairs of the club in the interests of all players and members and not in the interests of any one section. But if 2.5 per cent of its members think that money spent convening a special general meeting is better spent on printing, postal and hire charges and professional fees, then the General Committee, whilst strongly disagreeing, will have to incur such expenditure.

The General Committee hope that those members who attended the meeting at Ossett will reflect on what is being said in this statement. The General Committee hope that they, too, will reconsider their position as has the committee, and that in reconsidering the position they will bear in mind that the General Committee are entitled to manage and empowered to decide the management of the club's affairs and have been elected to do so, that there has been a great deal of dissension in the dressing room; that there is an urgent need to build a young, enthusiastic team all of whom will play for the team

*under the leadership of a player whose energy is
boundless, whose courage is never doubted and
whose character is typical of Yorkshire grit and
determination; and that what is needed from the
membership is wholehearted support of a new captain and a new spirit.*

Hear, hear, I thought. Well said . . . but it was never going
to work. It was exactly what the Reform Group expected, and
they started almost straight away. Norman Yardley and
Michael Crawford were so fed up they threatened to resign
as president and chairman and a special general meeting
was inevitably demanded, despite the committee's warnings
about the cost. They were going to hold it in December, but
due to some wrangling about who could vote and who
couldn't, who had paid their subscriptions and who hadn't, it
was postponed until 21 January. The results of that meeting
are history – a 1,006 majority to reinstate Boycott, 788 in
favour of a vote of no confidence in the cricket committee and,
worst of all, a majority of 31 for a vote of no confidence in the
committee itself. They had no choice but to resign and plans
were being laid for an election that made the General Election look like a show of hands at the parish council.

One thing I'll say for the Reformers, they were really
geared up for this very day. Their publicity machine clicked
into action to such effect that the committee were forced to do
something themselves. They took on a London agency to
produce a special bulletin to circulate to members before the
special general meeting in January, and though I was not
really involved and only went to one of the meetings, it was
obvious they were down to nine, ten and jack. The decent
guys of Yorkshire cricket had put all they had into the
county – many of them had nothing left. Look at Ronnie
Burnet – he was kicked off the committee in Harrogate by a
British Telecom employee named Roy Ickringill who admitted that his knowledge of first-class cricket was just about nil
and that he had only become interested at all because of the
Boycott affair. Ronnie told me that, because of Boycott, he

had been spending up to twenty hours a week at meetings. He was a senior employee of Hambros, the bankers and insurance people, and simply couldn't afford the time to canvass his members. His opponent visited just about every member in Harrogate, sat in their parlours, supped tea with them – yet Burnet was still beaten by a mere four votes.

The other two members of the peace-keeping trio were also beaten. Fred Trueman lost to Peter Fretwell by 63 votes in Craven and in Leeds Billy Sutcliffe polled only 365 votes against Tony Vann's 556. Luckily I'd seen the writing on the wall – I'd paid one visit to my accountant and taken myself off to Spain to await the inevitable.

It was a good job I did see my accountant. All my friends had gone and I knew it was only a question of time for me. I was going to sling it all in there and then, but my accountant asked: 'Have you any holiday due?' When I told him they owed me three weeks, he said: 'OK, take it then and let them finish you so they will have to pay you on your contract. There's no reason you should resign and not make anything out of it. You've made enough money for Yorkshire with your sponsorship deals and that. Don't be proud, just bide your time.'

I didn't have to wait for very long! The election was in March. Reg Kirk, who was already on the committee, held his place in Hull and became chairman. Within a couple of days he was trying to contact me in Spain to tell me I had been sacked – and what a botch he made of it!

I had left the number of a bar near our apartment with David Ryder, Yorkshire's assistant secretary. Joe Lister had got the number from David and he rang to leave a message that they wanted to speak to me. I arranged with some friends to take a call on their phone at 10 o'clock the next morning and I rang Joe to tell him. I asked him what was going on and he said: 'Sorry, I can't tell you. Mr Kirk wants to speak to you.' He couldn't wait until the next morning though; he rang my friends' number that same night, but I wasn't there. So he had to wait until the next morning when he broke the news to me. I asked him to keep it quiet until the weekend when we would be back as my daughter Diane was at home on her own and I didn't want her bothered or upset.

Kirk said: 'I can't. It's already out.' I was stunned. 'How d'you mean, it's already out?' I asked. 'It's only out if you released it.' 'Well, somebody's been talking – you know, to the press,' he replied. And at about the same time he was ringing me, a local radio station was on the phone to our house at home. Diane wasn't there – she was at work, so they called her there. Then Vicky, our other daughter, rang us from her home in Chesham to say that she had been speaking to Diane who was crying and really upset. I said: 'Ring her back and tell her I'll call her tonight. Tell her not to worry as this is what I wanted.'

But isn't that typical? They couldn't keep the news to themselves for three days. Certain members of the Reform Group were so jubilant they just had to tell somebody. They had to pay me off the year of my contract that was outstanding – and I was free at last! Of course, the rows at Yorkshire went on long after that – Boycott won a place on the committee which many people, including Brian Close, the new cricket chairman, thought inconsistent with his position as a player, etc., etc. And so it went on. But I must say that from my viewpoints on the Costa del Sol, from Woodhall Hills Golf Club, or the BBC commentary box, it all looks much more friendly than it did from my little office at Headingley.

And there were still the letters to keep my chin up . . .

I am so sorry – Yorkshire cricket is indeed going through a long, dark tunnel. One consolation so far as you are concerned is that you could not have been happy working with the present set-up – you have already suffered enough to last most people a lifetime.

All supporters of real Yorkshire cricket have cause to be grateful for all you have done for the county and for cricket in general. It will take Yorkshire a long time to recover from the damage that Boycott and his sycophants have done. He's a real

cuckoo in the nest [where did I hear that before?]
pushing out one after another of his rivals. I hope
you will be able to enjoy your retirement from the
county game, knowing that your fight for what was
best was appreciated by very many people.

Well, thank you, Mrs Joyce Kent from Bridlington, I am
enjoying my retirement very much. I was also interested to
learn the truth about a little incident that had been bother-
ing me for some time – yet another example of the Reform
Group's 'dirty tricks' campaign. It was Mr Ian Jones, of
Barnsley, who told me this one:

I attended almost every day of Yorkshire cricket last
season so I know just how few of these people,
especially Kirk, Slicer and Hellewell, actually
watch themselves. I also saw many incidents of
abuse directed towards you from some of their
supporters, including a member from Market
Harborough, who placed an abusive letter on the
windscreen of your car, anonymously signed of
course, and was very proud of the fact afterwards.

Mrs Jessie Wharton, from Middlesbrough, sent me a long
letter written in beautiful copper-plate which I cannot hope
to print in full. But the way she started off was enough:
'Could a complete stranger who is not even a dyed-in-the-
wool cricket fanatic offer a few words of support? The events
of the past few months must have left you, amongst many
others, wondering if there is any sanity left in the world, or at
least that part of it which Terry Wogan had dubbed: "The
People's Republic of Yorkshire".'
My friends rallied round too. The Yorkshire League sent
this:

It is the unanimous wish of the League that I should
write and convey to you our regret at your recent
displacement from the position of cricket manager

of Yorkshire County Cricket Club by the newly
elected committee and our very good wishes to you
for the future. The Yorkshire League enjoyed working with you for the good of both the game overall
and both organizations, and it is sad the relationship should be so abruptly terminated.

Mollie Staines from Dewsbury, a Yorkshire lady who
supported Leicestershire, wrote to say:

I suppose it was a question of time – and I've always
felt that you were to be the scapegoat . . . the one who
came back and was not appreciated – especially
when you 'dared' to criticize one G. Boycott, surely
the saddest person who ever walked on a sportsfield
– one wouldn't call him a sportsman. I want you to
know that I appreciate and know what you have
done since you came back to Yorkshire. I also bet
you have never been given the credit, especially for
the money side – the sponsorship which has come
Yorkshire's way – I do know as a Leicestershire
member how much you did there! – and I am glad I
have kept my Leicester membership. It's always nice
to escape to pleasant pastures!

Keith Moss is chairman of Pudsey St Lawrence and was
involved with a couple of companies through which I raised
some sponsorship for Yorkshire. He is an old friend, so it was
good when he wrote to me: 'I am dreadfully sorry about the
way things have turned out over the past few months. It
must give you, in some way, a great sense of relief that you
are out of the sorry "squabbles" that, regrettably, are going
to continue for a long time.'

There were many, many more – like the one from the
elderly gentleman in Scarborough, whose name I couldn't
even make out, who said he had supported Yorkshire since
the Twenties and went on: 'Now the treatment you have
received from Yorkshire makes me ashamed of the county.

In addition to the managership, and perpetually being abused by people who ought to have known better, it couldn't have been easy to resume playing, with the added responsibility as captain, when you were over fifty. You did a grand job.'

I reckon that's not too bad an epitaph, is it? He did a grand job. I didn't think I did too badly. Nor did some of the members who resigned over my sacking, like John Drake, of Newport Pagnell, who wrote to Joe Lister with his resignation: 'I believe the new committee has been thoroughly high-handed in their sacking of Ray Illingworth – at great expense if the press are to be believed. A man appointed to lead and whose leadership was undermined by rank sedition within the club, leaving him in an untenable position . . . it is no longer a pleasure to support Yorkshire but a great heartache to watch the club tear itself to pieces.'

Thank you one and all – from one man Yorkshire tried to tear to pieces and failed.

11

THE JOB OF
ENGLAND MANAGER

Right through the years there's only ever been one way for me to do a job: my way! That's how I have to carry out any job I approach and that, basically, is the reason I could not come to an agreement with the Test & County Cricket Board when they offered me the position of England team manager towards the end of the season in 1986.

Don't think I didn't believe England needed a manager. I knew to my own cost how much a Test captain could do with a man to take some of the weight off his shoulders. It's just that the way the Board looked at the job was not the way I viewed it – not by a mile. If I told you that one of the manager's duties, according to them, was to check the team's baggage in and out of tour hotels, you may have some idea of why I knew it would never work – not for me, anyway!

I just hope Micky Stewart, the present manager, can come to terms with the people at Lord's better than I could. And I hope he can prevent a recurrence of one particular Saturday morning back in 1973 when I was skippering England against the West Indies at Edgbaston. They were a few hours that still make me shudder and confirmed in my mind for ever the opinion that England have to have somebody in charge – only I mean *in charge*.

That was the famous occasion when Arthur Fagg refused to come out and umpire because he had been in a row with Rohan Kanhai the previous evening. So instead of preparing to go out and play a day's Test cricket in front of a packed

Saturday crowd, I spent an hour on the phone trying to prise somebody from Lord's off the golf course and ask them what the hell I should do.

In the end Alan Oakman, the Warwickshire coach, stood for one over and then Arthur, having made his point, agreed to return. A major row had been narrowly averted, but the fact remained that I, captain of England, had not even changed when the time came to go out on the field because I was still on the phone trying to sort out a problem that should have been left to a manager. The trouble is that the men at Lord's are still reluctant to give up their control, which is why they don't want to give a manager any real power. I felt desperately sorry for a decent guy like Tony Brown who was supposed to be manager of that terrible tour to the West Indies at the beginning of 1986 but didn't have the power even to order the players to go into the nets and practise.

That's why I knew things would have to change one hell of a lot if I was to accept the job when it was offered to me, even though I am sure that at the time, despite some things that have been said and written, I was the only man actually to be interviewed by the TCCB. I do know for a fact that David Brown, the old England fast bowler who is now manager of Warwickshire, was never asked. One paper even quoted him as saying he was not interested anyway – but only a couple of days later David told somebody at Yorkshire that the question was never likely to arise since he had not even been approached.

In some ways I can say that I was never really approached either, even though I seemed to be the man they wanted to speak to. It was all done in the usual bumbling Lord's way and it finally came to my notice that they wanted to talk to me when a member of the Executive Committee happened to ask me if I had spoken to Raman Subba Row, the Board chairman, yet. That was during the third Test against India at Edgbaston early in July 1986 and I had to answer, 'No, Raman hasn't said a word.' But by then that Test was well under way and I hadn't heard a word from Raman, so I thought I had better sort a few things out for myself. It was obvious Raman wasn't going to approach me so, instead of sitting in the sun outside the radio commentary box, which I usually did when I wasn't on air, I decided to go to the Warwickshire committee room for a drink with one or two friends who had invited me down there.

As luck would have it, there in the committee room was Raman. He sort of sidled over to me and asked, 'Do you have a few minutes to spare?' I said I couldn't talk to him then as I was due back on the air in a few minutes. He asked if we could arrange a meeting which, as it was quite late, we agreed to do the following day.

We fixed the meeting for 2 o'clock in that big bar they have at Edgbaston and that was how it happened. I just have the feeling that if I hadn't gone into that committee room to meet a couple of pals, nothing would have occurred. It didn't look as if Raman was going to make the effort even to see me, even though several Executive Committee members had made it clear to me that he had been told to get in touch.

I had taken a bit of trouble tracking Raman down, but after a few minutes I began to wonder if it had all been a waste of time. We spoke for the best part of half an hour, but he didn't really seem to have much to say. I thought he would come up with some kind of offer, but that was far from the case. We just waffled on about what my ideas about the job were and what their's were, and all we ended up deciding was that we would probably have to have another meeting. I can remember my thoughts; I couldn't help hoping any new meeting would produce a darned sight more than the one we had just concluded!

That new meeting came one week later during the Benson & Hedges Final at Lord's. Donald Carr, secretary of the TCCB, suddenly appeared in the commentary box and asked me if I could find time to see Doug Insole, who is chairman of the Board's Tours Committee. I agreed and popped down to see Doug at the close of play.

I was already beginning to form the opinion that this was not the job for me – what with the World Cup in India and

Pakistan, followed by a tour of Pakistan in the offing after Australia. That meeting with Doug just about settled it. He made it pretty clear that the terms and conditions they were offering could never match up to my idea of what the job should be. And he said some silly things like, 'Of course, when the tour manager is checking the hotel bills, we'd want you to give a hand with the baggage.' You begin to think: 'Am I going out there as team manager or am I going as baggage man?'

So I thought I'd check a few other matters as well, like the disciplinary side of things, for I probably wouldn't, initially anyway, have a say in the selection of the side. I asked him what would happen if, say, Ian Botham went on the tour and we had problems with discipline. He said he hoped we would be able to get on well together, but I said that sounded fine, but they had already called him to Lord's half a dozen times on disciplinary charges and the situation wasn't going to become any easier as he grew older. Doug said if there was any trouble he would expect me to go to the tour manager. When I asked what would happen if I didn't receive any backing from the tour manager, his reply was the same – he just expected and hoped I would. But the fact was that if I didn't have the support of the tour manager I would be a laughing stock – a long way up the creek without a paddle.

That just about put the mockers on it as far as I was concerned. I was already convinced they had the wrong idea about the job at Lord's. They shouldn't have been looking for somebody to trot along cap in hand with a tour manager over him; they should have been looking for a manager, pure and simple, with somebody like Geoffrey Saulez, who used to be the scorer, and is also a retired accountant, to take care of bills, hotel accounts and that sort of thing. If I had taken on the job I would have wanted complete power – selection, discipline, accommodation, the lot – just as Bobby Robson has for the England soccer side.

Then, if things go wrong, you know that you're going to be the one to carry the can. That's only fair. But how can you exert any control over the players on a tour if they know it's not up to you to make the major decisions? I don't know the conditions under which Micky Stewart has accepted the job, but if they are anything like the ones put to me, I would think he is taking a bit of a risk agreeing to them.

There is, of course, one area where I would happily hand over control – and that is to the captain on the field. I accept that, but I do believe that a lot of the cricket policy and the way you're going to play, should come from off the field as well. But I didn't see any problems there. I get on well with Mike Gatting. He is a straightforward sort of bloke and he sees cricket much the same as I do.

All these things were still going round in my mind when I ran into Donald Carr again at Lord's, this time during the first Test against New Zealand. He wanted me to have another talk with Doug, but I refused. I said I didn't want any more meetings. We had already held two and by then they must have known my feelings – or they certainly ought to have done. I asked them to put the offer down in writing – salary, what the job entailed, authority – and I would consider it. In the event I wasn't given very long at all. I ran into Donald as I was coming down the steps from the commentary box – he was obviously on his way up to see me. He had all the details written down and gave them to me, asking me to have a look and give him an answer by half-past five. It was half-past one then – after three weeks of mucking about they had left me with four hours to make up my mind.

But Donald was insistent. He said that if I was interested in the job he wanted to fix a meeting the next morning with Raman, Doug, Peter May and maybe A. C. Smith. Anyway, I had already talked with Shirley and neither of us was particularly happy about it; apart from the reasons I have already given, it would have meant giving up our winter holidays in Spain, which had become an important and welcome part of our lives.

So at half-past five I went down to see Donald Carr to tell him I was not going to accept the job. He asked me to tell Raman Subba Row, who was in one of the executive boxes at

Lord's. I said I couldn't see him right away because I was due back on the air, but I agreed to see him at the end of the day. That's what I did. I told Raman basically what I had told Donald and he said, 'Fine, thanks very much for telling us.' I went back to the Westmorland Hotel where I had a quiet dinner and neither saw, nor spoke to anyone except to pass the time of day. So you can imagine how annoyed I was to read all about it in the *Daily Mail* the following morning. I've told Donald Carr about this since and he says he didn't think it was in the paper, but I've told him to go back over his papers and check because I can assure him it was. I'll tell you how I know. The next day I was back in the commentary box and a fellow who always sits in the same seat, just behind the box, said, 'I see you've turned it down, then.' I said, 'Yes, I have. But how do you know?' He said, 'Well, it's right here in the *Daily Mail*.' That's when I decided to write about it the following day in the *Daily Mirror*, which they were not too happy about at Lord's. But that's their bad luck. It was them who told the *Daily Mail*. As I said to Donald, there were only three of us who knew about it and I certainly hadn't told anyone. That left him and Raman Subba Row, so they could draw their own conclusions about what had happened.

Having discovered that there is life beyond Yorkshire, I can now once again look down on the cricket world from my ivory tower – and I don't always like what I see. On the international scene I'll stick my neck out and say it's a downright tragedy that South Africa are almost permanently barred from Tests when other countries are doing things which, in a cricket sense and never mind politics, are unforgivable. Like any other sane-thinking man, I have no time for apartheid – but the South African cricket people have never made life hard for our players, which is more than can be said for a lot of the countries that England still play against. Joe Pamensky, the secretary of the South African Cricket Union, has done all he can to have his country accepted back into the fold of Test cricket, but as soon as the International Cricket Conference (ICC) made the voting 4–3 in favour of the black countries with the introduction of Sri Lanka he knew he was beaten.

Any trouble with South Africa, like the Basil D'Oliveira business in 1968, has been caused by their government, not their cricketers, which is more than you can say for some of the problems with the West Indies. At the ICC they veto everything that doesn't suit their style of playing the game – short-pitched bowling and over rates being their favourites. They are very cynical – not the slightest bit interested in the good of the game . . . only in their own success. And I'm afraid that Clive Lloyd, popular man though he is, might have done more in that direction when he was wielding a battery of four fast bowlers in every match to weld together the greatest 'mean machine' in the history of the game.

If we can't do anything about it when we go there, at least England should make sure the game is played properly when the West Indies tour here. We should tell them – when you come here we bowl 90, or even 95 overs in the day – that is our condition. You send them the conditions in advance and say: 'This is how we are going to play. Let us know within a week and we'll chat over any points you may have, but after that these conditions are final.' They'll have to like it or lump it. Even if they don't come at all, it would be better than watching them pounding down 12 overs an hour.

It's all about attitudes, and I'm afraid there are too many of the wrong ones creeping into cricket. I'll talk about sportsmanship in a minute, but right now I'm feeling unhappy about the attitudes of so many of the England players. We have let them reach the stage where they are running the game and doing more or less what they want. There's no doubt about that . . . it's got to get back to where a player just goes out and plays; that's his job, not to run the whole show. That's the manager's job – or should be, because I know that the job Micky Stewart has taken is nowhere near to being the position it ought to be.

Micky must have accepted roughly the terms that I turned down last summer. Really he has no proper say in what goes on. He must be hoping that by working from the inside he will earn himself more influence. I wasn't prepared to take that risk and do it for two years hoping to work myself into a position of control. I think that if you do a good job, and the team becomes better and better, there's even less chance of your being given more say. The people at Lord's would think: 'We're doing OK as it is, so we'll leave things as they are.' But if you're not doing very well, they'll give you the sack anyway. It's a hiding to nothing. You don't mind coming in and saying: 'If I have all the power I want and things don't work out, then I deserve the sack.' But I would expect a couple of years to mould things the way I wanted them.

In some ways it should be easy since you have the best players in the country at your disposal. You should be able to have your choice of every type of player you want. OK, we don't have any leg-spinners around; but you can pick a good slow left-armer, a good off-spinner, some reasonably good quicks, with plenty of time to sort out the ones you really want, and the best five batsmen in the country. So it should be easier than at county level where you are probably lacking in some departments.

But there will still be problems with the bowlers. We are at last finding a few lads who are willing to run in and try to bowl fairly quick. But captains don't know how to handle them. One day last summer I read in the paper that Neil Foster bowled 20 overs on the trot for Essex – how do they expect him to bowl a bit sharpish when they use him like that? In fact, I've never seen Foster bowl well for England. It's one thing to take wickets on those grassy tracks down in Essex. It's quite another to do it in international games. John Lever was the same. I never saw him as an international bowler and I'm not sure that Foster is either. Gladstone Small, Phil de Freitas and Graham Dilley are all pretty useful, and so is our own Paul Jarvis, who might have gone to Australia but for a back injury. But after that you're struggling, though I think England should have taken Greg Thomas. The Aussie tour is the place for a young quick to work and improve, but what annoys me is that Bob Willis had him for an entire tour in the West Indies and he came back with all the same faults that he went with. The lad's line is bad, which is why he doesn't take as many wickets as he should. Line, length and pace – they're the three ingredients, but line is the main one – get that right, plus at least one of the others, and he could still come through, though at twenty-six he'll have to do it soon.

But for me the saddest problem is the death of the spin-bowler, and that is something the England manager will have to face in a couple of years when Phil Edmonds and John Emburey have had enough. You have to have them in Tests and if they go out of cricket an important part of the game will have died. When you go back to the 1950s nearly every county had a leg-spinner and certainly a couple of finger-spinners. If you take out Pat Pocock, now retired, Norman Gifford and Jack Simmons, both in their forties, there's precious little left – except perhaps for Nick Cook, who had to leave Leicestershire because they wouldn't bowl him, and Rodney Ontong, of Glamorgan, who would have been my choice for Australia as a spinner who can bat. Yes, if I had become England's manager, my first priority would have been to find some bowlers and encourage conditions in schools and clubs where they would emerge. I'll tell you more about how I tried, and failed, to do that in Yorkshire. Then I'll tell you some of the other changes I am sure Micky Stewart would like to see, despite the successes he achieved in Australia.

12

SPORTSMANSHIP

I tried all I knew to persuade the leagues in Yorkshire to adopt policies which would have brought about the re-birth of slow bowlers – but it was hopeless. I told them that all the while Yorkshire stuck to their belief in using only players born within the county it was up to them to produce their own players. They couldn't go outside the county to find spinners, so if they didn't produce their own, they simply wouldn't have any. I told them that for me it would take away half the game itself if spinners went out of cricket. Yet they buried their heads in the sand: they couldn't see any further than the ends of their noses.

Yet I can remember when every side in the Bradford League had a couple of good slow bowlers. The first thing you asked when you were getting your side together was: 'Who is our slow left-armer?' But as I went round the leagues all I got was: 'Why should we change? We're the best league in the world.' It was unbelievable. 'OK,' I would say. 'Have you got a decent slow left-armer in your league?' They would say they hadn't and I would reply: 'Then how can you say you're the best league in the world?' All they've got is a string of tiddly medium-pacers and the better clubs were signing up a couple of good bowlers and letting them bowl all the way through the innings. It used to take about two and a half hours to go through the 50 overs – now it's taking up to three and a quarter hours because the two bowlers have to pace themselves.

I'm not against limited-overs cricket in itself, but I told the league officials they had to make the teams bowl 18 or 19 overs an hour. If they don't do that – OK, penalize them 10 runs an over for a year or so. I know it's artificial, but it has to be done to get the over rate right. Then there is no reason why they shouldn't bowl 65 or 70 overs each. If it's a match of, say, 130 overs, the side batting first should not be able to bat more than 70 overs – and I don't think any team will find two bowlers able to perform throughout an innings that long. So they will have to bring slow bowlers back again and try to get people out. That's how it was when I first played in the Bradford League – I wanted to take a wicket with every ball. Now it's: 'How do I stop him scoring?' That's why they're not developing bowlers in Yorkshire any more – and I'm sure it's the same throughout the rest of the country. And it shows right through to the highest level – sometimes I think Ian Botham is the only bowler in England prepared to take risks in order to bowl people out.

So that, above all else, would be my first priority if I were in Micky Stewart's cricket boots as England manager. I won't call him 'supremo' because the chaps at Lord's don't seem to like that word, probably because it suggests that he is in charge – and that's the last thing they want. It might mean losing some of their own power – and that would never do.

Like it or not, they do need somebody in absolute charge – and this is how he should operate. He would need a staff – probably a couple of men of his own choice working under him. They would most likely be coaches or old players who can go and watch players he wants information on. He would also have a network of people around the country that he knows and trusts to keep him up to date on everything that's going on. The manager and the two others would be enough full-timers – but they would have to be paid to give them status and respect. It shouldn't cost any more than the present system. You could find a couple of good blokes for not much more than the selectors are costing now in expenses and one thing and another. On tour you would do away with the need for a manager in the way they have one now, so the actual cost overall should not be too much more than it is at present.

Obviously, whoever did the job would be going on the tours. Part of the problem now is that the selectors who pick tour parties hardly ever see them play and have to rely on reports from the manager and the captain. But I don't see that the manager would have to be there for the whole tour – there would be other duties for him to perform. He would need to be there for the start of the tour to see that everything was functioning smoothly and then he could leave it to the captain. That would give the captain more responsibility, which is a good thing, while the manager would go off to watch cricket in another country. He might go and watch Australia play the West Indies, for example. That way he would see players performing at Test level and he would be able to advise England on anything he learned. Some players have been sprung on us recently, but that wouldn't happen if the manager did his spying properly, taking notes and watching players in Test conditions where you know they will be playing at full steam and not acting about. It would be very, very helpful to both batsmen and bowlers if the manager watched their future opponents for 15 or 20 overs.

He would be able to say to his spinners: 'This fellow hits everything on the on-side, the only shot he plays on the off is this – say a little dab to anything short.' That way you can arrange your field placings right from the word 'go' which is vital. You put pressure on them, so they can't score runs, and maybe they get out in frustration. On the other hand, if you take half a dozen overs to work out a new batsman, he will have 15 or 20 runs and he's going . . . it's a whole new ball game. But if you can turn the screws from the very first ball of the first Test it makes a big difference. The new batsman may get out once or twice. He loses a bit of confidence and he might never make a big score in the entire series.

I noticed the difference when I went back to playing with Yorkshire in 1983. There were a few players I didn't know, blokes who had come into the game since I finished with Leicestershire and I hadn't seen while I was a manager. I would ask the other Yorkshire players: 'Where does this fellow hit it?' and all I got was a sea of blank faces. There was no advice forthcoming – not even from Geoffrey Boycott. I'm not sure if he knew the answers or not. If he did, he certainly wasn't telling me!

The manager should also be setting up more trial matches, like the one at Edgbaston between a TCCB team and the New Zealanders. It would give him a chance to see eleven of his best young players all operating under identical conditions, something you don't have when you just watch them in various county games. For the same reason, I wouldn't be against a return to something like the old England trials, which were discontinued some years ago. The manager and his two assistants would be at the games for the full three days – not like the TCCB match at Birmingham. Peter May was there for three-quarters of an hour on the final day, Phil Sharpe was there for three-quarters of the first day, Fred Titmus did a bit on the second day and I suppose Alan Smith had a look whenever his duties allowed him outside the Warwickshire office. All four selectors should have been there for the full three days – it's either a full-time job or nothing at all. That's why I think B tours are a good idea, like the one to Sri Lanka in 1985–6. The manager would fly in to have a look as often as he could, but I would probably put the entire tour under the command of one of the manager's two assistants for an expert assessment of the players involved.

There is another sphere the manager could get stuck into – but only if he knew he was on a more or less permanent assignment and would have time to establish his theories. That sphere is the question of sportsmanship, an area where attitudes have changed since I first came into the game – and not always for the better. When I first went into Test cricket you walked. When you knew you were out, you went. It was as simple as that and it was drilled into us. The strange fact about cricket is that the sportsmanship grows worse as the standard of play declines – unlike soccer where Sunday afternoon matches on the park often pass off without a single foul, whereas First Division games are often a disgrace.

When I first played in the Bradford League nobody walked – they always waited for the umpire's decision and they still do. That's the way league cricket is played up here. Only last season I saw a fellow run out the non-striker when he was backing up. That's the way it's played. And in many ways I admire it because at least it's honest. Nobody walks so you don't expect them to. It makes it far more simple.

So it was something of a culture shock for me when I first went into county cricket in 1951 to be told by people like Norman Yardley and Brian Sellers: 'If you get a touch, you go!' That's how it was in the early 1950s, but by the end of the decade changes started to occur. People learned to walk when it suited them – when their team were 320–3 and they were over 100 not out – but not when things were a wee bit tight.

No, I'd rather have a bloke who never walks. You know where you are then and when I reached international level and became the England captain, I told the rest of the lads: 'I don't mind whether you walk or not. But you've got to be consistent and I won't stand for anybody showing dissent with the umpire's decision, whichever way it goes.' Unfortunately, I'd only been captain a few months when we embarked on the Ashes tour of Australia in 1970–71. That was when we were forced to adopt a non-walking policy, pushed into it by the fact that at least two or three decisions per match were going against us. This was because we were walking and the Aussies were just standing there and getting away with it. Even when we tried to stand there we were giving ourselves away by taking one instinctive step towards the pavilion before thinking and stopping. Eventually we got it right and by the end of my international career I was standing there and waiting for the umpire's finger – but it was a pity and I was only doing it because we had been forced into a corner by Aussies like Bill Lawry and Keith Stackpole (Stackie).

Lawry was the king. You could knock out all three stumps

and he'd stand them up and start again. One thing I had against Bill. It was in 1968 when Colin Cowdrey was still captain of England. Bill had made 135 against us in the first innings of the final Test at The Oval – the one we won when Derek Underwood bowled them out after a storm flooded the ground. Bill was given out caught behind by Alan Knott (Knotty) off John Snow (Snowy) to a ball which flew through chest high in a tangle of gloves, bat, the lot. Bill stood there and made a big fuss. 'I never touched it,' and all that stuff. I went up to him afterwards and told him: 'I don't appreciate all that, Bill. I accept that you don't walk even if we knock all three over, so if you're not going to help the umpire at all you have to accept whatever decisions you get – whichever way they go.'

Stackpole had two knocks every time he went in against us in 1970–71. I was laughing with him about it when the Aussies were in England in 1985. He admitted then that all the decisions that had gone against us had really been out. We just had to grin and bear it, but what really annoyed me in Australia was that you had to shout, even for a catch so obvious that everyone in the ground knew it was out.

Snowy had Stackpole in the first over of the Melbourne Test. It hit his glove and lobbed up to Knotty. It wasn't a flyer that might or might not have touched the glove – it lobbed at least five feet in the air. It was so obvious we didn't even appeal until we saw Stackie still standing there. Then we had to say: 'Well, how's that, then?' but that sounds so lame coming almost a minute later. After that we certainly shouted for the ones we knew were out – even if they were so obvious we would normally not have bothered. The problem with the Stackpole incident was that Max O'Connell, now one of Australia's best and most experienced umpires, was standing in his first Test and was so relieved to negotiate the opening over safely (or so he thought) that by the time we appealed he was already more than half-way to square leg.

Even today I think most English players would have walked for that one, but in Australia you have to let go with such a shout that the umpire is convinced he ought to give it.

Neil Hartley was never afraid to do what
he knew to be right, and he should have
been Yorkshire's captain for as long as he
chose

David Bairstow was as keen as they come –
but his keeping stopped him from
becoming a good captain

Geoff Boycott and ghost writer Terry Brindle put their heads together for
some hard work – by a hotel pool in Australia!

Reformers (left to right) Sid Fielden, Tony Vann, Geoff Boycott, Peter
Charles and Peter Briggs look happy enough here as they chalk up
another victory – but all too soon it turned sour for them

Some of the men who stood up against the Reform Group: (from left to right) Fred Trueman, Billy Sutcliffe, Desmond Bailey and Ronnie Burnet

Micky Stewart gets stuck into the job that I turned down – directing England operations on the 1986–7 tour in Adelaide

The finish of the most famous cover drive in cricket – Len Hutton cracks another boundary, this time against India in 1952

Below left: Ted Dexter could be devastating, even if I did get him a few times early on in his career!

Below right: Fred Trueman was a shire horse who simply never knew when to give up

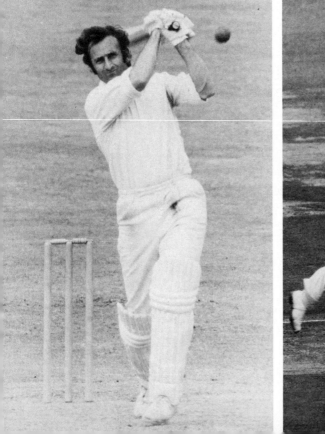

Mike Gatting was the type of captain I could have worked with if I had become England's manager

John Edrich had a terrific temperament and was a good bloke to have on your side when the going got tough

David Gower has a marvellous record, but I just wish he had worked a little harder on his game

Ian Botham and I have had our differences but he seems to be happy
enough here with (left to right) Graham Gooch, Mike Gatting and David
Gower

Below left: Where did that one go? Ian Botham, in his old Somerset
sweater, watches another six sail high over the ropes

Below right: Just one last look back as I walk off a county cricket ground
for the very last time after being bowled by Essex's Norbert Phillip at
Chelmsford in September 1983

Brian Johnston – with a shirt like that it's a good job he's a radio commentator!

What a line-up . . . the BBC Test Match Special team. Back row: Tony Lewis, Henry Blofeld, yours truly, Chris Martin-Jenkins, Peter Baxter, Bill Frindall; front row: Don Mosey, Trevor Bailey, Brian Johnston, Fred Trueman and Tony Cozier

Before and after. This is how I looked in my last year at Leicester – before the worry lines of five years at Yorkshire set in!

It could just be the wind, or did I really end up tearing my hair out during those years

But that's for the ones you are certain of. What amazed me in the summer of 1986 during the Tests in England against India and New Zealand, when there were at least two or three dodgy decisions, was that everybody was going up together – even for ones that were nowhere near out. I don't see how you can get six men round the bat going up together unless they've arranged it beforehand. It was amazing how all six were going up if there was anything remotely like a bat and pad.

I wonder what their answer would have been if a batsman had asked, as he should be able to do: 'Did you catch it?' I always felt that if somebody had asked me that question, as they sometimes did, and they felt they couldn't trust me if I said I had, then the game wouldn't be worth playing any longer. Never, never would I lie about a thing like that and nor would anybody I ever played with.

There were some pretty special people amongst them – men like Roger Prideaux and Arthur Milton. Prideaux was playing one of his first games for Kent against Yorkshire when I bowled him a ball which ended up in Brian Close's hands at silly mid off. Neither Close (Closey) nor I thought much about it and I was back at the end of my run for the next ball when I turned round and saw Prideaux half-way back to the pavilion. He must have got the finest of tickles on to his pad and from there into Closey's hands – but Brian had no idea Roger had hit it and nor did any of the other Yorkshire players except wicket-keeper Jimmy Binks, who said later that he thought he'd heard something, but nothing to get excited about. Basically, if Prideaux hadn't walked we wouldn't have appealed and he would have remained.

Milton was another. I remember getting him caught at short leg off his glove when we were playing Gloucestershire. It lobbed up and looked so obvious to all of us that for a moment we didn't appeal. When we saw Arthur still standing there we did appeal – but by then it was too late and the umpire said 'not out'. It was clear that Arthur hadn't felt a thing, and at the end of the over he walked down the pitch and asked me: 'Did I hit it, Raymond?' I said: 'Yes, it went off

121

your glove.' He just said: 'Oh.' But next over he ran down the pitch to me, took a swing, and got out. That's how cricket used to be played.

And it's no good playing it any other way. If you cheat, or if you make a scene over umpires' decisions, you're only going to upset people and it doesn't do you any good. I've had bad decisions like anyone else – but there are proper ways of making your point. The captain in county cricket marks the umpires at the end of each match and if they continue to receive bad marks, they don't get too far. You get nothing for showing off and, anyway, it only puts the umpire's back up against you and your team.

13

TALKING ON THE
AIR

I have confirmed my strong views on how the game should be
run through my work as a commentator with the BBC. That
was one of the things that softened the blow when Yorkshire
bowed to the politicians and fired me. Nick Hunter, the BBC
television cricket producer, had always told me there would
be a place for me in his team as soon as my playing career
came to an end. All I had to do was let him know when I was
ready.

So that's what I did, opening up a new career which gives
me about fifty or sixty days work each year – all I need at my
time of life, and, incidentally, something the Test & County
Cricket Board were expecting me to give up if I took their
manager's job without giving me any guarantee of employ-
ment for longer than the Australian tour.

The great thing is that commentating on Tests, the one-
day internationals and the later stages of our domestic
knockout tournaments, has kept me in touch with the first-
class game and all my friends in it. More than that, it has
brought me back into the Test scene which I had to drop out
of when I stopped playing for England in 1973 and started
to concentrate on county cricket, which took up all my time
in the summer.

I've been lucky to work for both TV and radio and people
often ask me which I prefer. It's hard to say – I love both. On
radio you have a little more time to chat away and expound a
few theories about what's going on out there in the middle.

But you have to be a lot more careful these days than you used to – many people have taken to watching the match on TV but turn down the commentary and listen to it on the radio instead. And they're not slow to pick you up if you say anything daft. On TV, on the other hand, you have that little monitor screen dictating to you and you have to get your timing spot on. It's no use rambling on when the bowler's about to let go of the ball.

Nick Hunter makes sure you do it right. If you don't . . . watch out! The professionalism of the BBC television people amazes me. The commentators wear headphones and we can hear everything the producer is saying. He will be quick to praise a cameraman who picks up a catch or a brilliant piece of fielding in the deep, but the air turns blue if anyone misses anything. If there's a lull in play and I decide to make a comment about, for argument's sake, Mike Gatting's captaincy, then woe betide any cameraman who fails to pick up a shot of Gatting wherever he might be standing in the field.

The commentators, though, are every bit as professional – even if every one of them on television has to be an ex-Test player to qualify. Those I've particularly enjoyed working with have been Jim Laker, sadly no longer with us, and Richie Benaud. Both were great professionals on the cricket pitch and they took that professionalism into the commentary box with them. The characters on radio are different and, with the exception of Tony Lewis and Henry Blofeld who won a Blue at Cambridge, none of the regulars has played first-class cricket. But they bring to the job another skill – the ability to talk and keep talking. Don Mosey, Henry Blofeld and Chris Martin-Jenkins all do a fine job in their own different ways, but my favourite has to be Brian Johnston – a terrific fellow.

It all goes back to my days as England captain when there was more than one press man not too pleased that I had been given the job and not too slow to voice that displeasure. But 'Johnners' was kindness itself, right from the start. He always treats everyone the same – whether they went to Eton and Oxford like him, or to Wesley Street Secondary

Modern, like me. That, for me, is the mark of a gentleman.

There's never a dull moment when Brian is around. He's no spring chicken, but he's still as enthusiastic now as he was twenty years ago, bounding up those stairs at Lord's or The Oval like a schoolboy. He also has the great gift of being able to laugh at himself – and he's the first to recount some of the gaffes he's made on the air. One I can remember concerned me . . . the time 'Johnners' said, 'And Illingworth has decided to relieve himself at the Pavilion End.' Or when he told listeners that Neil Harvey, that great Aussie fielder, was 'standing at backward short leg with his legs apart hoping for a tickle'.

Only one thing ever seems to bother Brian – I do hope that one day somebody will be able to put him out of his misery and explain exactly what a man he saw walking round Headingley while he was on the air was doing. The man was struggling to carry a long and heavy ladder and at the same time carrying a lavatory seat around his neck. To this day 'Johnners' worries about exactly where that man planned to put that lavatory seat!

It's 'Johnners' the radio people have to thank for all the cakes, too. The TV commentators have never discovered his knack of persuading ladies up and down the country to bake, pack and send them in by the box-load. We receive at least two or three every day and Brian has appointed me chief taster. I'll be growing fat if this keeps up much longer!

Commentating was a new experience, and obviously I'm learning all the time. One thing it took me no time at all to learn, though, was how touchy today's Test stars have become. Perhaps it's all the money they earn, but I can't understand how they can so easily resent the honest, unbiased opinions of men like Richie Benaud, Ted Dexter, Tom Graveney – apart from Yours Truly – all of whom, may I remind them, have played this game a bit themselves.

It first came home to me during a Test at Nottingham in 1983 when I was replying to some questions about Ian Botham. I made it clear I didn't want to criticize anyone, but I did say that I felt that if Ian took a look at a film of that Test against Pakistan at Lord's in 1978, when he took 8–34 in their second innings, he would see he was in a quite different position when he bowled in those days than he is now. His left shoulder was a lot further round and that's why he was swinging the ball away a lot more. He must have been told what I had said – there are always people only too happy to dash off and tell the players what's been said about them but only the criticism, not the praise, of course. They never seem to hear the good things, even though we are more than ready to give praise when it's deserved. But that was when Botham first started to get the hump with me – the most I can expect ever since is a brief grunt if we pass each other in the hotel or at the ground – yet the TCCB expected me to handle him on a tour without giving me any authority!

But whatever he thinks, I am happy in the knowledge that if there is any ill feeling between me and Botham, then he was the one who started it! Back in 1983, my last season as manager of Yorkshire, he wrote in that erudite column of his in the *Sun*, that he thought we were a 'Mickey Mouse' outfit. Later that season we won the John Player League on a terrible day at Chelmsford when it rained all day and not a ball was bowled. So the Yorkshire lads sent him a telegram: 'Weather fine in Disneyland. Wish you were here. Love, Mickey Mouse.' So, if he wants the truth, that's when it began – he's quick enough to dish it out, not so ready to accept the flak when it's flying in his direction. It's such a shame. When he's done things right, I'm the first to praise him, but he doesn't want to remember that. So it's only fair if I get stuck in when Botham, or anyone else, plays badly – like he did at Lord's in 1984 when David Gower asked the West Indies to make 342 to win in five and a half hours. Botham let Gower down that day, taking 0–117 in only 20.1 overs; Gordon Greenidge made 214 not out and the West Indies strolled it by 9 wickets. Yet in the first innings Botham had taken 8–103 and bowled beautifully – and I said so at the time. You have to take the rough with the smooth in this game of ours, and I'm afraid a lot of them aren't prepared to.

Say what you like about Geoffrey Boycott, but I know that he, sensitive to criticism though he can also be, would have been on the phone to the BBC the next morning asking to have a copy of the video I had been talking about so he could check whether what I had said was right and what he could do about correcting it. That is a professional for you!

14

UP WITH THE BEST

Talking of contrasting attitudes, it is fascinating to compare the players of today with those of the recent and even more distant past. But first let me say one thing . . . I don't think and never have thought that cricket is all about stars – it's a team game. The main factor that enabled us to bring back the Ashes in 1970–71 was our team spirit. We weren't the best team in the history of the game and often we were working on a shoestring when it came to filling various positions in the side. But we went a record number of Tests, twenty-six of them, without losing and twenty of those were under my captaincy. I remember when that run came to an end. It was against India at the Oval – the third Test in 1971. We had to bowl them out for less than 173 in the final innings to keep that record and I remember Brian Luckhurst coming up to me and saying: 'You've worked a few miracles, but if you win this one it will be the biggest of the lot.' We got six of them out before they made it, but it was very tight and with a bit of luck we might just have scraped home. We certainly gave our all in that match and it brought home the truth of what I had always believed – if you have everybody trying their hearts out the whole time, you don't lose a lot of matches and you're always in with a chance of winning.

We didn't have any real awkward characters when I was captain – if there had been any they wouldn't have been playing anyway. I think that's the answer – you just don't have them. John Snow could be a little difficult at times, but that was mainly because of the treatment he had received down at Sussex. Once I got Snowy sorted out with some man-to-man talking – what I expected from him and what I would do for him in return, we became very good friends and still are. Snowy would work his backside off for me, and he was one of the best. None of the quicks I've played with bowled any better than Snowy did on that Australian tour – and that includes Fred Trueman, Brian Statham, Frank Tyson – the lot. He ran out of steam a bit towards the end, but that was understandable with all the Tests we were involved in.

Snowy wasn't built like Trueman. Fred was a Shire horse; Snowy was a whippet who needed to rest and build himself up. Yet we went from Melbourne to Adelaide with only a day's rest between Tests and he had lost half a stone bowling in the heat at Melbourne. Can you imagine John Snow losing half a stone? He didn't have half an ounce of surplus fat on him at the best of times.

But of all the quicks I knew, Fred kept going the best. Brian Statham always tried to give all he had and bowl as quick as he could. Fred had to pace himself, but when you think of the number of overs he had to bowl, anything up to 1,200 in any one season, that's understandable. When you look at how many they bowl now – if they reach 500 they reckon they're being murdered – you could see why Fred had to take it easy at times. He would bowl off a short run and swing it and still take wickets that way because he had such a perfect action. Statham was a big help as he would do all the donkey work into the wind. He was the same whether he bowled into the wind or with it; but I've seen the wind switch while Fred was bowling and he would either want to change ends or he didn't want to know.

When it comes to batsmen there's only one – and nothing to do with the fact that he was my boyhood idol, that I nearly got a whacking at school for sliding off to watch him bat, or that I was born considerably less than a million miles from his home town of Pudsey – that's him . . . Len. I think Sir Leonard Hutton, to give him his full title, was a class above all the others. But for the damaged left arm, shorter by half an inch than the other one after an operation caused by the war, Len would have broken every record going. He was forced to play his cover drives in such a side-on position that it must have been a hell of a handicap. Later in his career he sometimes had to bat with his left arm strapped. Many times he had to use a Harrow bat, but he was still in a class of his own.

Of the moderns, the batsmen who played all their cricket after the war, I rate Peter May as the tops. He had the toughest mental attitude of them all; he wouldn't just let you bowl to him, he wanted to dominate. Once Peter had been in ten minutes or a quarter of an hour you had to bowl well or he'd whack you all over the place – unlike Colin Cowdrey, who could be tied down, even on a good pitch, if you bowled anything like properly at him.

Ted Dexter was another fine player. For a long time he didn't have the defensive technique on a turning wicket, though he did improve later in his career. I did Ted for three or four noughts earlier in his career, but on a good wicket he was a devastating player – particularly in Test matches. I don't think anybody ever hit the ball harder than Ted, and you can include Botham in that if you want, but he never achieved all that he might have done. His attitude to everything was too easy-going, and he gave the game up too early as well.

Garry Sobers was a marvellous player on all kinds of wickets – he could play on everything and do everything – two types of bowling and even keep wicket if called upon. You probably had a better chance against Garry if it was moving off the seam a little – but who couldn't you say that about? Again he was so dominating and the greatest West Indian I ever saw, though I must admit that I came on the scene about the time that Frankie Worrell and Everton Weekes were leaving it.

You've also got to admire Geoff Boycott because of his defensive qualities, but I'd never put him down as a great player because he never dominated. A truly great player makes the game – Boycs always sat back and allowed the game to come to him. But definitely he was the best manufactured player there has ever been. Defensively Len may have been a shade better, but there's not much in it, yet Boycs fell short of greatness because of his attitude and his fear of failure.

John Edrich was a good player too. He was a great batsman in that he never allowed anything to upset him – least of all the ball that went before. It was like Fred Titmus once said: 'I get fed up with beating him twice an over and still finding he's taken eight runs off the other four balls.' John had a marvellous temperament – he was a good bloke to have on your side, especially at Test match level.

Of the present-day players, I suppose the one I know best is David Gower, since I was still at Leicester when he came into county cricket in 1975. What disappoints me about David is that he has not worked a little harder at his game. He has a marvellous Test record and there is no better player to watch when he's going well. But he's still got the same faults he had when he first arrived at Leicester. It's all very well for him to say that he'll make his share of runs when things are going well, but if he had worked just a little bit harder – by gum, he'd have been a good player. It's too late now. He should have started putting things right ten years ago when we started working on him at Leicester . . . but he hasn't stuck at it. When I first saw him he couldn't play spin bowling to save his life, but luckily we had some pretty good nets at Leicester that wore a bit and gave the spinners a chance to get something out of them. So David had myself, Jack Birkenshaw, Chris Balderstone and John Steele bowling at him for hours and it was amazing how much he improved in the first twelve months he was there.

If only he had kept on doing that for another year – and at the same time brushing up his defensive technique, against the quicks as well as the spinners. There are times when you just need to stay at the wicket and if David had been able to master that side of batting he would have a Test average of 50 or 60 today. But you'll never get him to change now. He still plays as though his feet are tied together and that's a thing that should have been sorted out years ago. There are a lot of little things; David still plays too low to the spinners. I would always bowl to him with a man just behind square and when he hits it that way he hits it up and is so vulnerable there when he first comes in. I'm afraid Gower has never had the ambition – that's what has let him down in his batting and it is what let him down as captain. To be a good skipper you have to concentrate for six hours a day every day. You can't drift off for half an hour now and then because by the time you drift back again the game can have gone for ever.

Mike Gatting (Gatt), of course, has less trouble with the spinners than most. He's a tough little so-and-so and he doesn't show the slow bowlers any mercy at all. When he's going well he can murder them, coming down the pitch to whack them for six or waiting for them and laying back to cut them for four if they drop short. But Gatting's domination of the spinners leads to one of the main faults in his captaincy – and John Emburey and Phil Edmonds agree with me on this. Gatt sometimes thinks spinners just can't bowl and for that reason he tends not to use them in Tests as much as he should. That's the difference between Yorkshire and Middlesex – we were brought up on the idea of having an off spinner at one end and a good slow left-armer at the other. Apart from Fred we've never had a really fast bowler, just a number of useful medium-pacers and we would use fielders to pressurize people and to keep them quiet on good wickets.

15

FARSLEY CRICKET CLUB – MAN AND BOY

My chance to go back and play for Farsley came in 1984 – and I jumped at it. I would have gone sooner if I'd had the opportunity. But 1984 was my first season out of top-class cricket since 1950 and my only chance since then of going back to where it had all started for me when, at the age of fourteen, I had made my bow in Farsley's 2nd XI. I'd never wanted to play for any other club than Farsley and, apart from a couple of games as a stand-in while I was on the Yorkshire staff, I never have. Even those games had been forced on me as I would much rather have played for Farsley when I didn't have a game with Yorkshire. But the Bradford League had a rule at that time that county players could not turn out in their competition, which I thought was pretty daft as the presence of professionals can only raise the standards and the interest of the game.

I'm glad to say they've scrapped that rule now, but at the time the only way I could find a game was once as a substitute for West Indian Conrad Hunte for Enfield in the Lancashire League and once for Leeds in the Yorkshire Council when they were short.

It has been a real thrill for me to take stock and realize what a new lease of life I have had since returning to Farsley. It is strange how, after a lifetime with Yorkshire and Leicestershire and leading England to the Ashes, I can now find as much excitement and fun in the achievements of a small, but happy, club in a little West Riding village. I suppose it's all a question of where your heart is – and if I ever look like forgetting that mine is in Farsley, then there's a little black and white photograph hanging over the club bar to remind me. It is of me, in crumpled second-hand cricket gear, taken in the first week of June 1949 – the week I reached my seventeenth birthday. Behind me is the Farsley scoreboard showing a total of over 350 with one batsman 148 not out.

That batsman was me, at the end of a week-long Priestley Cup struggle against Pudsey. It was like a timeless Test – each side batted until they made 150, then the others had a go until they reached 150, and so on. I batted most of the week and at the end they had a whip-round among the crowd, which could be anything up to a couple of thousand people. I made £23, which was a small fortune in 1949, and I spent it on kitting myself out – bat, pads, clothing, the lot. It was amazing what you could buy for £23 in those days – no more crumpled cast-off gear for young Raymond Illingworth!

I had had my first taste of Farsley when the club, always on the lookout for young talent, used to let my school play on their ground at Red Lane as we didn't have a pitch of our own. My great idol then was Len Hutton – what else would you expect from a Pudsey lad? But it was Farsley who held out the hand of friendship and it was there that I learned a lot of my cricket from all sorts of players, but mostly the older, more experienced ones. Jackie Firth, the Leicestershire and Yorkshire wicket-keeper, was Farsley's pro in those days and I listened a lot to him. Donald Waterhouse and Harry Bailes were two others – neither of them had played professional cricket, but they had spent their lives in the leagues and there wasn't much they didn't know.

A couple of evenings a week I used to lend a hand rolling the wicket – and it's amazing how much you can learn from the old hands just chewing the fat as you trudge up and down behind the heavy roller. I wish some of our youngsters would do the same these days – talk about the game until it comes out of their ears. Ninety per cent of cricket is what goes on in your head – but the lads these days always seem in too much of a tearing hurry to stop and think. They don't know what they're missing.

I must admit I did have a few misgivings when Farsley asked me to go back and play for them again, even though it didn't take me long to make up my mind. When you get in to your fifties the old aches and pains seem to come more quickly and go more slowly, though I was heartened by the fact that I had gone through the previous season as captain of Yorkshire without missing a game through injury, mainly by sticking strictly to our stretching exercises.

So I made one good decision at last – I said 'Yes', even though I knew that after skippering England and Yorkshire I might find it a little different to go back into the leagues and play under an amateur captain, especially one who, as it turned out, had never skippered a cricket team in his life! That was the case with Brian Hird, who was captain of Farsley in 1984, my first year back there. I didn't go back as captain, by the way. They're canny folk in Yorkshire – I've no doubt they wanted to see if I knew anything about the game before they took the risk of making me skipper! And I can honestly say that, but for an unfortunate illness of Brian's wife that forced him out of the game, I might never have been.

You see, Brian was good. Very good. He had played a lot of decent football and skippered a number of teams, so he knew what leadership was all about. He would always listen if I had any suggestions to make and often he would come up and ask my advice. He was intelligent, a keen and brilliant fielder – and what I liked was that he wanted everyone else to be able to field as well. Brian and I thought along the same lines there. He was a marvellous catcher, yet every time we had a practice session he would have twenty or thirty catches hit to him until catching became second nature. He knew he was going to hang on to just about anything within reach and that's exactly what happened, just because he was confident. If you've caught a few dozen balls in practice you know you're going to catch anything that comes your way in a match. It makes such a difference when you actually want the catches to come to you, when you can shout 'Mine!' as soon as the ball goes up in the air without looking round and praying it's going to someone else. But if you've dropped a couple, and you haven't been catching them in practice either, you become a bit apprehensive.

I've certainly enjoyed being captain of Farsley for the past couple of years. I feel I've picked up where Brian left off. I find I still have something to pass on to the youngsters. You only take out of this life what you put in. I've taken a lot out of cricket and this is my way of putting a bit back in. I find it hard to understand ex-Test stars who cut themselves off completely from the game that has given them so much once they are too old to play and earn from it. Over the years I've learned a way of doing things in a pretty hard school and all I ask is that people respect what I've learned and try to see things my way. That's what I told them at Farsley before I agreed to be their captain. I'm happy to say, to a man, they agreed . . . that all the time I was in charge we would play cricket properly. That's hard, but fair and we would enjoy the game and have a drink in the bar with the opposition afterwards – win or lose!

We've had two marvellous, happy seasons since I took over there as captain. In the first one we just about beat the record number of points for the league, but still only came second to Pudsey St Lawrence, our great local rival. They had a good season and managed to make up on us when bad weather was about, and they played and we didn't. It was a pity those games weren't at home, because the Farsley ground is on a slope, like Lord's, which helps it to dry easily. It's on the top of a hill, too, and we always say that if we can't play at Farsley because of rain, then nobody else is going to play either. At the end of a season that can make all the difference between winning a league and ending up nowhere. Still, Pudsey did beat us when we met, so I suppose they deserved to take the title in 1985. We were pipped in the Priestley Cup that year, too. We lost by 8 runs in the semi-final when both our openers, Ashley Metcalfe and Mark Chadwick, who plays for Lancashire, had to cry off.

Last season looked well on the way to being a disaster before it had even begun as we had lost both our opening bowlers by the end of April! One was an Australian named Lennie McKeown who turned up for the start of the season and within a week had gone back home again. That was a bit annoying as we had him for the previous season and he had been happy, had a marvellous time and took about 90 wickets. He went home for the winter, came back again and within a week said he wanted to go home again . . . so that was the end of one fast bowler. Then Richard Thorpe, who had been at the Yorkshire nets all winter and was a pretty useful medium-fast bowler, decided the pressure was too much for him and cleared off to play for somebody in the Halifax League – more as a batter than a bowler, I'm told.

That gave us almost no chance to find a replacement, but I dashed down to Headingley and signed Paul Jarvis and Simon Dennis, hoping that at least one of them would be available for most of the season. As it turned out, Jarv played well for Yorkshire and we didn't get a single game out of him while Simon played six or seven games, which was useful, but we could have done with a lot more.

As it was, we had to make do with the bowlers we had in the second team or what we had left in the first team. We pushed David Brown into opening the bowling and he did very well for us, largely because of his experience – he's thirty-seven now and has played a good number of years for Farsley. Then we had Peter Vallance, who bowled left-arm seamers and batted as well, but he packed up three-quarters of the way through the season because he said the pressure was getting to him. And then there was Michael Proud, a young lad who used to go to the Yorkshire nets when he was fourteen and I was still manager. But he was only sixteen and he hadn't bowled at all for two years – so that was our seam-bowling attack for you. On top of that, we didn't see Ashley Metcalfe at all and Chadwick could only manage about half our matches. So not only had we lost both our opening bowlers, we had to do without our opening batsmen as well for most of the season. I was able to play only half the games, so we did well to stay out of the bottom three and finally end the season with about six other clubs below us.

I still do a bit of work on the Farsley ground like I did in the old days and I have to admit that I enjoy it. I keep my hand in with the garden at home: the lawn is always trim and I like to keep the place neat – it's the hard grind of making it neat and tidy in the first place that I'm not so keen on!

All the time I'm doing my little bit of work on the ground, I'm dreaming up ways of making the boundaries a few yards longer. Back in the old days I was mostly a batsman, and if I bowled it was the medium-pace seam-up stuff. So I wasn't too bothered if the boundaries were on the short side – yet if there is anything about the club I would change now, then that is it! All the grounds in the Bradford League are on the small side, which is something I find hard to understand since most of them were laid out at least 100 years ago when land must have been cheaper and more plentiful than it is now. Everybody uses 3 lb bats these days and if they take a swing at you it still bobs over the line for six even if they don't connect properly. It's quite a problem for a slow bowler, especially as a few of the lads still like to go home and tell the wife how they hit Ray Illingworth out of the ground! Still, I can't stop them having a dart and there are times when I stand there watching in dismay as the ball lobs over the head of the man on the edge when on a county ground he'd be running in twenty yards for a comfortable catch.

Peter Gott and John Cockshott are the two lads who do most of the work at Farsley and I just help them out. Even the chairman Dick Storr works hard – cutting the grass, keeping everything tidy and generally making sure everyone is happy. Dick does a lot for the club, and he and I have become good mates. He is a friendly sort of chap and that rubs off on the club itself. That's been terrific, because even when I've been away Shirley has always felt welcome there and she can go for a drink and a natter with the people she knows. Diane goes to Farsley a fair amount too, as she is married to Ashley Metcalfe, the Yorkshire batsman who is also a member of Farsley.

As captain I've been on at the lads a lot about fielding. Sometimes, these days, the young players don't pay enough attention to it. Even when they come to nets they tend to take a ball each, eight people bowl then they all bat and then they either clear off home or into the bar. They really ought to spend at least half an hour on all aspects of the game. I had to do it when I was a colt and it's sad they don't do it now. Fielding practice, properly organized, can be fun, anyway. One thing's for sure – it's certainly no fun to spill a catch in the last over of a match when you need one wicket to win and you haven't been to a fielding practice since before you can remember. Mind you, I can talk! With me, these days, it's more a question of 'Don't do what I do, do what I say.' Obviously, I don't practise as much as I did, but at the age of fifty-four I reckon I've done my bit.

I find my bowling action has settled into such a groove after all these years that I don't have to work on it too much. I can still bowl pretty well from memory and it doesn't take me too long to work out where to bowl at any opposing batsman. I don't have to bat too often for Farsley so I'll carry on playing as long as I can still bowl. I've told the chairman I'll review the situation each year and that's how it stands at the moment. It may not be Yorkshire and England any longer, but I'm back where it all started – playing in the First Division of the Bradford League for Farsley – and thoroughly enjoying every minute of it.

16

A PLACE IN THE SUN

From being Raymond Illingworth, object of hate and abuse, target of obscene phone calls and victim of lies – all in the name of Yorkshire CCC – I'm now Raymond Illingworth CBE, captain of Farsley CC, BBC commentator and man of leisure. And I love it!

I own a holiday home in the Spanish sun; I no longer leap into the air like a short leg when some bloke bowls a long hop every time the phone rings; and three rounds of golf a week have brought my handicap down to 10, and if I carry on the way I'm going it could soon be a lot lower. Seve Ballesteros . . . watch out!

If it's starting to sound as if life is treating me well . . . then that's right. It is. But I reckon I've earned it. I was happy with Yorkshire during the 1950s and 1960s when we were all good mates, even if, as I've said, we did used to bicker more than somewhat now and then. It was Leicestershire through the 1970s and that was also a marvellous ten years. But then came my return to Yorkshire as manager in the early 1980s and, frankly, you could never call them happy years. There was too much controversy and too much nastiness. Now Shirley and I can go out in peace and have a meal with friends without being constantly pestered. We can do without all that aggravation and it's good to be able to do what we want while we're still young enough to enjoy it.

The door to today's life swung open at the end of the 1983 season when Yorkshire, as I've already said, waited until they were sure I had left for a holiday on the Costa del Sol, and only my daughter Diane was at home, to announce that I was no longer their manager. The rebels had won, for the time being anyway, because, as we all now know, their turn was yet to come.

It was ironic that Yorkshire should wait until I was safely tucked away in Spain before pulling the lever on the trap door, since it has been in Spain that Shirley and I have found it easiest to relax, forget and try to forgive. We've had a two-bedroomed apartment at Playamar, just outside Torre-molinos, for the past ten years. It's really swish – so good that if we could find an apartment like it anywhere near Leeds we'd snap it up and live there. But in Spain they build with an eye to the sun, and there's nothing quite like it around Pudsey where I was born, brought up and still live.

Our apartment is in a complex with everything you'll ever be likely to need – including that sunshine. There's tennis, swimming pools, a big restaurant, crazy putting and table tennis – all outside in the midst of beautiful gardens. Though I say it myself, it's nice . . . very nice. Our apartment faces south so we can enjoy the sun all day long – in the middle of January we can sit on the balcony, read a one-day old English paper, eat our breakfast and sunbathe at the same time. I do love Yorkshire and always will – but the West Riding in January was never quite like this. What the heck? I'm not a professional cricketer any more, so it's about time Shirley and I did what *we* want. And that is to spend most of our winters out there in Spain, whereas before we had to make do with a week here and a week there. It's not such a bad idea when the years start slipping past and the cold of an English winter begins to bite deeper . . . and deeper.

I belong to the Campo de Golf, which is really the Malaga Golf Club. It's what we'd call a municipal course in England, but out there it's quite different from what we're used to. It's about 7,000 yards long and is a really good test of golf. On top of that, the course is only a mile or so down the road from where we live, which makes it all very handy. I know quite a few people – mostly English, but with some Canadians and others mixed in, who either have apartments near us or else take regular holidays out there. Several of them play golf and most of them have to drive past our place on their way from the town to the club, so I'm usually OK for lifts!

There are about eight fellows who play off handicaps somewhere near the same as mine, so we can regularly fix up a couple of four-balls and be sure of some reasonably tight finishes. The great thing, though, is the weather. You can arrange to play and be quite sure that's exactly what you're going to do – not like dear old England. Afterwards we go to a little Spanish bar owned by some friends of mine and a few drinks round off a very pleasant day. You could say golf has become an important part of my life – I took it up about twenty-five years ago when I packed up playing soccer regularly and started looking round for something to keep me fit during the winter. In Spain I play on Monday, Wednesday and Friday, something I wouldn't like to have to guarantee at Woodhall Hills, my own club near home.

Shirley doesn't mind either – in fact I think she loves it . . . gives her a chance to get rid of me for a few hours! She doesn't play herself, but I think you could definitely mark her down as the Merry Golf Widow. One of the great things about Spain is that we have built up so many friendships there – like Janet and John White, who own a pub called the Sun Inn only a few yards from our apartment. They come from Manchester, but they've settled in Spain permanently now – they say there's less rain there than in Manchester! If they do come back to England for a holiday, like at Christmas, they usually stay with us which is nice, as it gives us a chance to pay them back for their hospitality to us in Spain. Shirley can always pop in their bar for a coffee or a drink when she goes shopping. Or she can go into Nick's Bar instead – that's run by a chap from Sussex. It's all so relaxed – that's what we enjoy most about Spain after the tensions of those years with Yorkshire. And if it's sunny, which it usually is, Shirley is quite happy to wash her hair while I'm playing golf and then sit on a sunbed and read a book for a couple of hours while it dries.

Yes, life has changed quite a bit for us – and for the better. At least I can thank Yorkshire for that. I'm glad things have quietened down – it's given Shirley the chance to become used to not having Vicky and Diane around the house any more now that they are both married. We don't see Vicky much at all now; she's living down south in Chesham after marrying a chap named Peter Philpott – not the old Aussie Test player, incidentally! But he does work for Guinness, so he should come in useful now and then – especially at Christmas! Actually, we're very lucky. Shirley misses Vicky a bit, but Peter is a nice lad – he must be, he plays a spot of cricket and Rugby Union as well.

His biggest ambition seems to be to beat his father-in-law at pool, but I've given him fair warning . . . no chance! You see, that's another game I play quite a bit in Spain. There's a table in one of the bars and every week they organize a tournament which gives me a chance to top up my supply of gin when stocks are running low.

Talk about the sporting life! What with the cricket back at home, I'm happy to say I'm a pretty active all-rounder. Only one favourite game seems to be forgotten – and that's bridge. At least once a week when I was at home I would have a few friends round for an evening session that developed a habit of going on for most of the night. All that seems to have dropped off. And to think that Brian Close, Phil Sharpe, Tony Nicholson, Richard Hutton and scorer Ted Lester used to join me in a regular school in the Yorkshire dressing room. But there I go talking about Yorkshire again. I thought I'd got them out of my hair once and for all! But you never do . . . With all this, I have at least got the bad times with Yorkshire out of my system. The bad times, but not Yorkshire: I had many good times there, and I now remember them with more affection than ever.

INDEX

Index